Lies We Believe
About *God*

Also by Wm. Paul Young

Eve

Cross Roads

The Shack

Lies We Believe
About *God*

Wm. Paul Young

**SIMON &
SCHUSTER**

London · New York · Sydney · Toronto · New Delhi

A CBS COMPANY

First published in Great Britain by Simon & Schuster UK Ltd, 2017
A CBS COMPANY

1 3 5 7 9 10 8 6 4 2

Simon & Schuster UK Ltd
1st Floor, 222 Gray's Inn Road
London WC1X 8HB

www.simonandschuster.co.uk
www.simonandschuster.com.au
www.simonandschuster.co.in

Simon & Schuster Australia, Sydney
Simon & Schuster India, New Delhi

The author and publishers have made all reasonable efforts
to contact copyright-holders for permission, and apologise
for any omissions or errors in the form of credits given.
Corrections may be made to future printings.

A CIP catalogue record for this book is available from the British Library

Scripture quotations marked AKJV are taken from the American King James Version. Public domain.

Scripture quotations marked ASV are taken from the Authorized Standard Version. Public domain.

Scripture quotations marked BSB are taken from The Holy Bible, Berean Study Bible, BSB Copyright © 2016 by Bible Hub. Used by Permission. All Rights Reserved Worldwide. Source http://berean.bible/terms.htm.

Scripture quotations marked CEB are taken from the Common English Bible. Copyright © 2011 Common English Bible.

Scripture quotations marked DBT are taken from the Darby Bible Translation. Public Domain. BibleGateway.com.

Scripture quotations marked the ESV® Bible are taken from The Holy Bible, English Standard Version®. Copyright © 2001 by Crossway, a publishing ministry of Good News Publishers. Used by permission. All rights reserved.

Scripture quotations marked Holman CSB are taken from the Holman Christian Standard Bible®. Copyright © 1999, 2000, 2002, 2003, 2009 by Holman Bible Publishers. Used by permission. HCSB® is a federally registered trademark of Holman Bible Publishers.

Scripture quotations marked KJV are taken from the King James Version. Public domain.

Scripture quotations marked NASB are taken from the New American Standard Bible®. Copyright © 1960, 1962, 1963, 1968, 1971, 1972, 1973, 1975, 1977, 1995 by the Lockman Foundation. Used by permission. (www.Lockman.org)

Scripture quotations marked NIV are taken from the Holy Bible, New International Version®, NIV®. Copyright © 1973, 1978, 1984, 2011 by Biblica, Inc®. Used by permission of Zondervan.

All rights reserved worldwide. www.zondervan.com. The "NIV" and "New International Version" are trademarks registered in the United States Patent and Trademark Office by Biblica, Inc®.

Scripture quotations marked SBLGNT are taken from the Greek New Testament. Copyright © 2010 Society of Biblical Literature and Logos Bible Software. Used by permission of Society of Biblical Literature. Source: https://www.biblegateway.com/versions/.

Interior design by Jaime Putorti
"Burn the White Flag" in chapter 2 is the title of a song by the band Joseph.
Unless otherwise noted, Bible quotations are paraphrases from the original Hebrew or Greek.

Trade paperback ISBN: 978-1-4711-5239-9
eBook ISBN: 978-1-4711-5241-2

Printed and bound by CPI Group (UK) Ltd, Croydon, CR0 4YY

Simon & Schuster UK Ltd are committed to sourcing paper
that is made from wood grown in sustainable forests and support the Forest
Stewardship Council, the leading international forest certification organisation.
Our books displaying the FSC logo are printed on FSC certified paper.

To Scott Closner, my best friend.
You were the first man in my life who told me that
no matter how badly I messed up, you weren't leaving.
Thank you!

To Tim, my brother.
You have lived a life of questions, mostly unspoken,
but questions about things that matter. You matter!
I love you!

Contents

CONTENTS

Lies We Believe About *God*

Foreword

Most Christians have a deep desire to be faithful to Scripture, as do most biblical scholars. Yet what constitutes faithfulness and how to achieve it is another question. Several months ago I read a book titled *Four Views of Hell*. Four scholars, determined to be faithful to Holy Scripture, presented four entirely different and certainly opposing views of the biblical teaching on hell. These writers believed they were presenting the true teaching of the Scriptures. I do not doubt the integrity of the four authors. But the differences in interpretation highlight the fact that something other than "reading the Bible" is involved. Very often the deepest question, and the one most ignored, is *how* to read the Bible. What does it mean to read the Bible correctly? How do we go about deciding?

Some of my friends laugh at such questions. "Baxter," they exclaim, "it is right there in plain English! Any honest person can understand what it says."

Yet the fact is, we all bring our family prejudices, our personal histories, and our habits of thought into our reading of the Scriptures. Just as we cannot hear our own accents, we cannot readily see our own assumptions—assumptions that shape what we see and how we see it. Not least this applies to what we "see" in the *plain* teaching of the Bible. It is important to ask ourselves questions about the way we read the Bible.

N. T. Wright's new book, *The Day the Revolution Began,* makes this very point. Wright carefully lays out what he believes to be the larger, biblical picture, what many call the metanarrative of the Bible's story, which then guides our interpretation of the details. His big picture leads him to seriously challenge doctrines long held as "plain and obvious" to us in Protestantism. Whether or not one agrees with Wright, his book puts us in a place where (like it or not) we can hear our accents, and at least notice our prejudices—prejudices that have a profound impact on what we consider "obvious."

My dear friend, Paul, has ventured beyond his wonderful and challenging fiction novels and here offers a more straightforward book about what he believes—*Lies We Believe About God*. This is a great book, but like *Four Views of Hell* and *The Day the Revolution Began*, it, too, has a very definite framework of assumptions. How does Paul determine what are lies and what is the truth? I can assure you, there will be places where some will throw up their hands and think, *Has the brother lost his mind?* When our understandings of the larger story of the Bible differ, then our beliefs about the details differ, too, and we "see" things differently.

So what is Paul Young's baseline? What are his core beliefs? How does he see the larger story of the Bible that so shapes his outlook and determines what he thinks is the truth and, therefore, what he believes are lies that need to be challenged? If you will allow me a paragraph or two, I will take you behind the curtain and lay out these beliefs as clearly and honestly as I am able.

For here, Paul and I are brothers who walk together, and what we believe informs the way we think about a wide range of biblical and human issues.

Paul and I agree that the New Testament explodes in the joyous conviction that Jesus Christ is the Lord God in Person. He laid down His life for the forgiveness of sin and to defeat the powers of death that enslaved humanity, and that as life incarnate, He rose victoriously from the dead. The gospels and letters that make up the New Testament are attempts to explore and express the meaning of Jesus's presence and death. The apostles, John and Paul in particular, realized the staggering implications of Jesus's very identity as the Son of God incarnate, crucified, resurrected, and ascended. Apostle Paul envisions Jesus as being with the Father before creation as the One in and through whom humanity is created and given the gift of grace (2 Timothy 1:9), and as the One in and through whom the Father chose us and predestined us to adoption before the foundation the world (Ephesians 1:4–5). The apostle Paul sees Jesus as the One *in* and *through* and *by* and *for* whom all things were created in the heavens and on the earth, the One who was before all things, and the One in whom everything is sustained and held together (Colossians 1:16–17).

For me and Paul Young, such thoughts are astonishing and worthy of the most serious reflection. Paul, the apostle, thinks of Jesus as there with the Father before the creation of anything, and he sees Jesus as the center of the divine plan for the entire cosmos. Indeed, he proclaims that Jesus's incarnate life, death, resurrection, and ascension is the summing up of all things in heaven and on earth (Ephesians 1:10). These are seriously radical ideas to almost anyone in the ancient and modern world.

The great apostle John agrees with Apostle Paul's astonishing vision and thinks of Jesus as the eternal Word of God, face-to-face with the Father before creation, and as the One in whom all things were created. John is emphatic: "All things came into being by Him; and apart from Him nothing came into being that has come into being" (John 1:1–3). Think about it. For the apostles John and Paul, and I suspect the others, we will never meet anything anywhere at any time that did not originate in and through Jesus Christ and is not constantly, moment by moment, sustained by Him. It is these core

beliefs about Jesus that formed the apostolic mind, in-
forming and re-forming their vision of God, of humanity,
and of creation, with the crucified and resurrected Jesus
at the center of all. Jesus himself declared, "I AM the
light of the cosmos, the one who follows me shall never,
ever walk in the darkness, but shall experience the light
of life" (John 8:12).

While there is enough here for us to understand
Young's basic framework, please allow me space to add
a touch of history. As the news of this Jesus—the crucified and resurrected Son and Creator—spread across
the Mediterranean basin and beyond, it collided with
existing cultures and worldviews, ingrained prejudices,
and habits of thought. The identity of Jesus Christ as the
Son of God, the One anointed in the Holy Spirit, *crucified and resurrected*, simply made no sense to people, and
the implications of His existence rocked the status quo
everywhere. The news of Jesus was turning the world
upside down, creating a universal, tumultuous writhing
inside human thought. Explosive debates developed,
even wars. Many believers were burned alive and crucified as martyrs.

FOREWORD

Who is Jesus, really? What does His existence mean? There were many answers. How could the apostolic vision of Jesus Christ not disturb the empire, whether the empire was external and systemic (religious and political) or internal and personal? The temptation to domesticate the Jesus of the apostles was ever present and convenient. In AD 325, bishops from the global Church were summoned to Nicaea (in present-day Turkey) to make a definitive statement about Jesus. The flamboyant and popular presbyter named Arius put forward the notion that Jesus was not God, not *really* God, but the first and highest of all God's creations, through whom all other things were then created. Bishop Alexander and others countered that the apostles taught that Jesus was God of God incarnate. Eventually the debate was "settled" as the council agreed that Jesus was *"of the same being as the Father"* (*homoousios to Patri*), thereby envisioning Jesus as the fully divine, incarnate, eternal Son of the Father and the Creator of all things in heaven and on earth, incarnate. It was this mystery—this culturally inconceivable proclamation that Jesus was of God's very being incarnate (confirmed at both the Constantinople and the Chalcedon Councils)—that was handed down as the central truth of all truths of Christian faith.

The implications of this confession are mind-boggling. If Jesus is one being with God and one being with us, then His very identity as fully divine and fully human speaks volumes about the relationship between God and humanity and about everything else in the universe. Was this union of the divine and human simply Jesus's plan B, a halftime adjustment, quickly thought up and implemented after the "surprise" of Adam's debacle; or are we here standing before plan A, the original and only divine plan? How seriously are we to take the absolute oneness between Jesus and His Father, and His absolute oneness with us as broken sinners? Are we not here in Jesus Himself standing before the greatest news in the universe? Is there anything that the union between the divine life of God and the human life of Jesus does not address? Is it wrong (from an apostolic and early Church perspective) to throw oneself into the pursuit of thinking out the implications of Jesus's very existence? Is not the union of Jesus and His Father the very light that informs us? Is it not the light of life? Or is it simply one among many other viable frameworks when it comes to thinking about the nature of God, about what it means to be human, about why Jesus died on the cross, about what we call social justice, and about our "global village"?

Athanasius, who accompanied Bishop Alexander at the Council of Nicaea, and later others, such as Gregory Nazianzus and Hilary of Poitiers, spent their lives defending the council's confession of Jesus's identity. From my perspective, working out the implications of Jesus's identity as the eternal Son of God united with humanity in our sin is the task of truly Christian theology. Here we find the metanarrative, the larger story from eternity that informs and re-forms our vision of God, of humanity and creation. What, for example, are we to make of the fact that this Jesus—the eternal Son of the Father, the one anointed in the Holy Spirit, the Creator and Sustainer of all things incarnate—was crucified, died, and was buried, and on the third day rose again from the dead, and then ascended to the Father in the Spirit? Are we to see ourselves, our enemies, the human race at large, and creation itself untouched by such a divine-human event? The apostle Paul proclaims that when Jesus died something happened to us and to creation. When this Jesus died, we too died; all creation died (2 Corinthians 5:14). And when Jesus rose, the apostle Paul sees that we all (who were dead in transgressions) rose with Him in life, and ascended in Him to the Father's right hand in the communion of the Holy Spirit (Ephesians 2:4–6). Such notions are not footnotes to Paul's more important teaching. They are fundamental to his and to the apostolic mind. Such a stunning vision of Jesus cannot help but have implications for the cosmos and for the human race, and not least for how we understand God. Again, is Jesus's life, death, and resurrection merely a plan B? Or is Jesus, as the Father's Son and anointed One and Creator and Sustainer of all things, and thus us all in Him—is He not the light that enlightens the darkness of our minds and the truth that defines lies?

After years of wrestling with the teaching of the apostles and with the writings of the leaders of the early Church, I can give you my thesis. It is not perfect, but it is honest, and I think it will help you understand where Paul Young is coming from. Here it is:

To speak the name of Jesus Christ with the apostles and with the early Church leaders is to say, "Father's eternal Son," and it is to say, "Holy Spirit, anointed One," and it is to say, "the Creator and Sustainer of all things—incarnate, crucified, resurrected, and ascended to the Father." Therefore, to speak the name of Jesus is to say that the Triune God, the human race, and all creation are not separated, but together in relationship. Jesus is Himself the relationship; He is the union between the Triune God and the human race. In Him, heaven and earth, the life of the blessed Trinity and broken human life are united. Jesus is our new creation, our adoption, our inclusion in the divine life, the new covenant relationship between God and humanity, the kingdom of the Triune God on earth.

You can see in my thesis why Paul and I regard the widespread notion that human beings are separated from God as a fundamental lie, one that denies Jesus's very identity. We are both committed to thinking out and communicating the implications of Jesus's identity in every way possible. The "lies" that this book set forward are perceived as lies through the lens of Jesus's identity and what His identity shouts to us about God, about ourselves, about creation, about our destiny, and about our future. When I read this challenging and liberating book, I can see Paul's vision of Jesus and hear him saying, "Therefore, God would not say this or act this way. Therefore this is a lie, or a misinterpretation." You may disagree with his conclusions, and I am not sure that I agree with all of what Paul says, but I know his intentions. He is standing in the mainstream of historic Christian confession about Jesus's identity, and he is attempting to work out the day-to-day implications of the very existence of Jesus Himself as the Father's eternal Son in His incarnate union with the human race in its darkness. And he is holding our evangelical feet to the Christological fire of the apostolic vision. Is not that at the heart of what it means to be faithful to Jesus Christ? I am proud to be with him in this endeavor.

Much more, of course, should be said, and that is what Paul is doing in this book. As you read, watch Paul's mind work. As he identifies a lie, ask what it is about

Jesus that would lead Paul to think that something is a lie. Watch him think and reason out of his beliefs about Jesus. Who knows, you may even catch him making a Christological mistake!

I know this: if you are willing to give Paul a fair hearing, you will find freedom and joy rising in your heart. It is not easy having your mind blown, but that is the way the apostles tell us we are set free by the truth.

C. Baxter Kruger, PhD, author of
The Shack Revisited and *Patmos*

Introduction

———————

The genesis of this book was a series of tweets I wrote called "Words you will *never* hear God say." I have a list of about 125 of these little statements, such as:

> *I keep a record of wrongs.*
> *You are the child I never wanted.*
> *I will let you keep your most precious lies.*
> *You overestimated Jesus.*
> *I need you.*

You get the concept. When we look at negative space (what God would *not* say), we can see the positive space from a different perspective. The exercise is often rude in that it might challenge our paradigms and assumptions, but that alone would be a momentous payoff. Potentially, it is an enlightening and helpful exercise. By looking at something God would *not* say, we are better able to examine ideas we have assumed to be true, often exposing lies we tell ourselves about God.

In my novel *Eve,* one of the characters makes a statement in the first chapter that has become increasingly significant to readers: *Choose your question carefully. One good question is worth a thousand answers.*

The world I grew up in did not place a high value on questions. At best, questions were a sign of ignorance and, at worst, were deemed evidence of rebellion. Anyone who disagreed with our theology, science, or even opinion was an enemy or a target. What mattered was certainty.

As I have aged, hopefully with grace, my life has been more about being open to "a thousand answers" than it has been about being right. It has taken me a long time to become a good hearer, one who isn't listening only in order to defend or declare, but one who allows a conversation to challenge and perhaps even change assumed ways of seeing.

In my younger years, I presented myself as a person of intelligence and rationality. This image allowed me to hide inside my ideas, trying to avoid the messiness of real life and authentic relationships. I used this persona as a defense mechanism and a safety wall to keep people at a distance. I thought I had fooled them. But it turned out that I was smart and creative, which empowered me to stay aloof and isolated and do damage to others through my words. You might have respected me for my persuasive argumentation, but you wouldn't have liked me.

Thankfully, I have changed a great deal. The inner house of my soul has been massively and painfully deconstructed, and my broken heart has undergone arduous reconstruction. But like the rest of us, there is plenty of "finish work" still to do in my own heart and mind, always being and becoming.

I was raised in a Western Evangelical Protestant tradition. There is no such thing as a pure heritage; the beautiful and edifying are entangled with the ugly and damaging. Half-truths, even lies, worm their way into our hearts. Like mold that has infected a work of art, this invasive darkness must be carefully removed so as not to damage the original and creative.

This book is not a presentation of certainty. None of the examinations of "lies" results in a final or absolute view on a subject. Rather, they are tastes of larger conversations. Each chapter refers to a statement I once believed and from which I have transitioned. You may identify with some and not with others. You might agree or disagree with my conclusions. Some of these ideas may be deeply challenging, while others may seem naïve and thoughtless. That is the wonder and uniqueness of our journeys and the beauty of dialogue and relationship.

If there is one man in Scripture with whom I most identify, it is the man born blind. My journey has been one of learning how to see, sometimes for the first time and other times with greater clarity. While I have studied widely, I do not have the depth of many theologians who have given themselves to specific texts and ideas. I am grateful for their work, and I read and listen to them as gifts.

What you are about to read will tell you much about me as a person. These rearrangements of my theology have not come easily, but they have impacted me for the better. Because of this movement within, I am a better husband, father, son, friend, and human being. If my words don't bring clarification, hopefully my life does. There are times when the only confession I can make is with the words of my favorite character: "I was blind, but now I see."

I would ask that you allow the words of this book to be both a friend and an adversary. The former because I don't want anything that is precious to you now to be less precious when you finish. The latter because we all need to have questions asked of us, of our assumptions and paradigms. Our prescriptions must be tested in order that we might have eyes to see and ears to hear. In the writings of theologians, philosophers, psychologists, and scientists, I have found both friends and adversaries; and I am better for listening and allowing their input to till up the ground of my heart and mind, to root out weeds, to plant seeds, and then to water those seeds— even bringing some to harvest. It is not always a "fun" process, but it is worth the work.

Ultimately, we are in this together. Your health is my health. Your loss is my loss. We often choose to believe a lie rather than allow the truth to invade the safety of our prejudices and self-protective fortresses. Dialogue ought not to be an exercise in domination or certainty; rather, it is the respect due relationship. We all need new ways to see. I know I do.

Again, this book is laid out as a series of essays exploring interconnected concepts that I propose are lies—lies that I once believed, lies that continue to affect many of us. My theologian friend Dr. C. Baxter Kruger, author of *The Shack Revisited, Patmos, Across All Worlds, Jesus and the Undoing of Adam, The Great Dance*, and more, has written a foreword that sums up the foundation of what I propose as Truth. Here Baxter beautifully frames this entire book.

For some, the concepts in this book will be new and transformative, uncomfortably so at times. Relax. The Holy Spirit is your true teacher; God, whom you can trust and who knows you completely, is trustworthy to lead you into the Truth, who is Jesus.

Again, I do not offer the following pages as complete

or final answers. The older I get, the more aware I am of what I don't understand. I offer these essays as ideas and questions to ponder, with the hope that our inner eyes will be touched and that we will more clearly see the goodness and relentless affection of God and who we are within that encompassing embrace.

1

"God loves us, but doesn't like us."

It is the middle of winter in northern Alberta, Canada. The temperature is well below zero, one of those days that is so cold your nose hairs feel like little sticks plugging up your nostrils and every exhalation of breath becomes its own fogbank. I was born not too far from this city, up in the northern prairies.

"At least it's a dry cold," someone offers, which is true, but not that comforting.

We enter the building and I unwrap the layers of protection, trading them for the warmth of this place of incarceration. We are visiting a women's prison. The women who have asked me to come and speak said that dozens of copies of *The Shack* have been making the rounds and having an impact. The government has given these inmates a "time-out," an invitation to think about their lives and choices, something that people outside these walls have little opportunity to do. These women are here today to spend an hour with me, by their own choosing. Their presence is a gift.

Those who have eyes to see will find much wonder beneath tough exteriors and callous hearts. Most of the women are here because of a relationship gone wrong, and their suffered betrayals and losses are visible in their bluster of defiance or barely concealed shame. I feel quite at home here, among the bruised and wounded. These are my people, our people.

I don't remember what I talked about. It probably had to do with the prisons in my own life, places that became precious to me because they were all I knew. About how we hold on to the certainty of our pain rather than take the risk of trusting anyone ever again. Deeply wounded souls in the room began to weep. Bruce Cockburn, the Canadian poet and musician, would call these "rumours of glory." Lost coins, lost sheep, lost sons, but not just any. These are *my* sons, *my* sheep, and *my* coins.

I finish my talk and only a few leave. Others wait to have me sign a book. I hug everyone, which I am certain is a violation of all sorts of rules. But I have been breaking such codes for a while, and no one ever interferes

"Do you really think," she whispers in short bursts, "that Papa is fond of me?"

with these sacred encounters. A woman stands waiting, her body tense with emotion. When I simply take her in my arms, it is as if I set off a charge that lets the dam burst. She sobs uncontrollably, for minutes. I whisper that it is okay, that I have other shirts, that I have her and she is safe. I can't comprehend all the misery and humanity that is flooding through this one small touch, but it is real and visceral and wrenching.

Finally, she stops the heaving enough to find some words.

"Do you really think," she whispers in short bursts, "that Papa is fond of me?"

And there it is, the question. This tender human being is entrusting me with this monumental question. Even those who don't believe that God exists are desperate to know that love does and that love knows who we are. More, we are driven from within to take the risk to ask of someone or Someone, *Do you find anything in me that is lovable, that is enough, that is worthy of being loved?*

There is a scene in *The Shack* in which the main character, Mackenzie, is having his assumptions challenged. Mack is face-to-face with Sophia, the Wisdom of God, and she is asking him about the love he has for his children. In particular, she asks which of his five children he loves the most.

Even moderately healthy parents would tell you this question is impossible to answer. My wife, Kim, and I have six children. When our eldest was born, we couldn't imagine ever having the capacity to love another child. Our first used it all up. But then our second arrived, and suddenly there was a new depth of love that either hadn't existed or had been dormant before his arrival. It is as if each child brings with him or her a gift of love that is deposited into the hearts of the parents.

"God loves us, but doesn't like us."

In the religious subculture in which I was raised, we all knew that God is love. We said it and sang it all the time, until it didn't mean that much. It was simply the way that God is. It is like the grandchild who says, "But you have to love me. You're my gramps."

But saying "God is love" doesn't capture our question, does it? So I've made a habit of rephrasing the line "God loves you," and instead of making it about God, I make it about the object of God's relentless affection—us. So throughout *The Shack,* Papa would say, "I am especially fond of her or him." There is a world of difference between saying "I love you," which is about me, and saying "I am especially fond of you," which is about you. Both are correct, but the latter somehow pierces the disquiet of our souls and says, "Yes, I know you love me, but do you know me and do you like me? You love because that is the way you are, but is there anything about *me* that is worth loving? Do you 'see' me, and do you like what you 'see'?"

"Do you really think," she whispers in short bursts, "that Papa is fond of me?"

I squeeze her tight. "Yes," I whisper back as we both dissolve into torrents of tears. "Papa is *especially* fond of you!"

Minutes later she regains a semblance of emotional control and looks up into my face for the first time.

"That's all I needed to know. That's all I needed to know."

With another hug, she exits, leaving me thinking, *Darlin', that is all any of us needs to know!*

2

"God is good. I am not."

This lie is *huge!* And it is devastating! So why is it so largely believed?

Many of us believe that God sees us all as failures, wretches who are utterly depraved. We've written songs to reinforce our assumptions, penning lyrics about our own ugliness and separation. We think, *When I hate myself, am I not simply agreeing with God?*

If we took the time to listen to one another's stories, we would discover that most of us have something in common—shame is the centerpiece of our self-appraisements. But we didn't get there alone. Some of us heard a constant barrage reinforcing this lie.

You are worthless.

You are stupid.

You are not valuable.

You are just dumb.

I hate you.

Why can't you . . . ?

You have made my life miserable.

You are trash.

You are damaged goods.

We then turned these messages into self-declarations, "I am not . . ." followed by a litany of our failures as human beings: "I am not smart enough, or skinny or tall or colored enough. I am not a boy; I am not strong; I am not . . ." We forget that every "I am not" began with an "I am": "I am worthy; I am smart; I am loved; I am . . ." But we even turn "I am" against ourselves, and follow it with another list of shames: "I am . . . a loser, a loner, bad, ugly, overweight, alone, dumb, worthless."

Is this how God sees me? Is this how God sees *you*? Does God agree with how I see myself and what others have told me about who I am at the core of my being?

"God is good. I am not."

Growing up with my father was too often terrifying. Being around him was like walking through a minefield, with the explosive devices changing positions every night while I slept. It wasn't all terrible. There were moments of kindness, attempts at being a loving father, but these were disconcerting in themselves. They felt like an invitation to let my guard down. I'm not making value statements about my dad: his "chip" for being a father was smashed by his own father long before I showed up. But when his switch flipped, when he went from absent to furiously present, I felt as if I were being torn apart and scattered to the winds.

My father was a missionary. He was the righteous man who was never wrong, and he was a strict disciplinarian.

I believed I deserved his anger, of course, because there was nothing good in me. I was being rightfully punished, even when I didn't have any idea what sin I had committed by omission or commission. I did try to defend myself, sometimes by lying, but when that didn't work, I resorted to three words, which I screamed over and over and over as the waves of his rage approached.

"I'll be good! I'll be good! I'll be good!"

What I have come to understand over the years is that with every scream of "I'll be good!" I was making a declaration to the core of my being that has taken me decades to unravel. That declaration was brutally simple:

"I am not good."

Only a few days ago I was speaking to a beautiful gathering of young people, high school students, who had invited me to be a part of "spiritual emphasis week" on their campus. They opened with a song that I am familiar with. Many of the lyrics are truth, but it begins with a massive lie.

[God] You are good, when there's nothing good in me.

The truth is that we have inherent value because we are made in the image of God. Our value and worth are not dependent on us. But those of us who are desperately broken and wounded may believe that if there is nothing good in us, there is no hope for real transformation. We think that the best we can do is some form of temporary self-discipline, a way to cover up our shame through façade and performance. All the positive speaking in the world won't change a rock into a bird of paradise. Many of us learn to fake it until we are completely exhausted from trying to keep all the lies spinning. Inevitably, the poisons in our inside-house begin to seep out in ways we can't control. Or we simply give up and act out what we have already determined about ourselves.

If I believe the deepest truth about me is worthlessness, then why are you surprised when I act like I'm worthless? Am I not at least being honest? Yes, I would be, if that were the truth about who I am; but it is not the truth.

Does anything that is "not good" originate in God?

No!

Are we still image bearers, made in the image of God?

Yes, we are!

God, who is only good, creates only good—very good! This is why Jesus asked the rich young ruler, "Why are you calling me good? There is only One who is Good, and that is God" (Matthew 19:17). This is not Jesus saying, "There is nothing good in me," but asking, "Do you see God in me, young brother? Is that why you are calling me good, or is this still about performance?" If you read the rest of that story, you will see that it is still about performance.

What would you think if you happened on a parent berating his or her child with these words: "The truth about you is that there is nothing good about you. You are sick and twisted and totally and utterly depraved. You have always been and always will be worthless. May God have mercy on your soul!" Sadly, there are some who think this is the "gospel," and worse, it is preached by people in positions of power behind pulpits.

> *God, who is only good, creates only good.*

Yes, we have crippled eyes, but not a core of ungoodness. We are true and right, but often ignorant and stupid, acting out of the pain of our wrongheadedness, hurting ourselves, others, and even all creation. Blind, not depraved, is our condition. Remember, God cannot become anything that is evil or inherently bad . . . and God became human.

Our children will always have an essential identity that is linked to us, their mother and father . . . forever. They have the potential to make disastrous choices, even harm themselves and others, but their core nature is an expression of us. It is who they are. Just as our identity does not exist independently, neither does our goodness. I am fundamentally good because I am created "in Christ" as an expression of God, an image bearer, *imago dei* (see Ephesians 2:10). This identity and goodness is truer about us than any of the damage that was done to us or by us.

God doesn't have a low view of humanity, because God knows the truth about us. God is not fooled by all the lies we have told ourselves and each other. Jesus is the truth about who we are—fully human, fully alive. Deeper than all the hurt and broken bits and pieces is a "very good" creation, and we were created in the image and likeness of God. But we have become blind in the deceit-darkness we believe. It is time for us to stop agreeing with these devastating lies instead of surrendering to them; it is time to "burn the white flag"!

3

"God is in control."

I was sitting in a hotel lobby in Orlando, Florida, having a conversation with my friend K, from Germany. Her world-class young athlete friend was recently paralyzed as a result of an on-camera stunt that went horribly wrong. K was distraught. She dried her eyes and said, "I struggle believing this is all part of God's wonderful plan."

So do I! Do we actually believe we honor God by declaring God the author of all this mess in the name of Sovereignty and Omnipotent Control? Some religious people—and Christians are often among their ranks—believe in grim determinism, which is fatalism with personality. Whatever will be, will be. It happened. And since God is in charge, it must be part of God's plan.

There is an impassable chasm (except perhaps in our darkened imaginations) between a God who takes owner-ship for the Creation along with the havoc we have pro-duced, and One who authors the evil itself. The first you might learn to trust, the latter . . . twisted lip service at best.

Admittedly, we humans are control freaks, wanting to control everyone and everything around us so that the things we fear won't happen. We inherently know that control is a myth, that one rogue cell or another person's choices can instantly change the direction of our lives, but we still fight for it and even demand it. So if we can't have control, we want a God who does.

How often have we heard the well-intentioned words, "It must be part of God's plan"? Really? Might it be that many things are simply *wrong*? There is no justification for much of what we have brought to the table, what has been done to us, and what we participate in ourselves. It is *wrong*! Wrong, wrong, wrong, wrong, *wrong*!

Yes, God has the creative audacity to build purpose out of the evil we generate, but that will never justify what is wrong. Nothing, not even the salvation of the entire cosmos, could ever justify a horrific torture device called a "cross." That God would submit to our darkness and then transform this dark machine into an icon and monument of grace speaks volumes about the nature of God, but it does not justify evil.

Does God have a wonderful plan for our lives? Does God sit and draw up a perfect will for you and me on some cosmic drafting table, a perfect plan that requires a perfect response? Is God then left to react to our stupidity or deafness or blindness or inability, as we constantly violate perfection through our own presumption? What if this is about a God who has greater respect for you than for "the plan"? What if there is no "plan" for your life but rather a relationship in which God constantly invites us to co-create, respectfully submitting to the choices we bring to the table? And what if this God, who is Love, will never be satisfied until only that which is of Love's kind remains in us?

One day I was working on a project with my four-year-old grandson G, though *project* might be too generous a term. We were attempting to put together a bookshelf, the sort you buy in a box, and trying to decipher the directions, which seemed to have been written by people who don't speak English. G and I had put almost half the bookshelf together before I discovered that I had built the first third backward and would now have to take it all apart and start over. G had been patient and involved throughout the entire process,

What if there is no "plan" for your life but rather a relationship in which God constantly invites us to co-create?

cess, but when he saw the look on my face, he knew something was up.

"Hey, Gramps, are you okay?" he asked.

"Yeah, I am, but . . ." And I proceeded to explain why I was now taking apart our work of art. "I am feeling . . ." I paused trying to find the right word. "I am feeling . . ."

"Exasperated?" he offered, all serious and compassionate.

I laughed out loud. "Thanks, G. That is exactly the word I was looking for, *exasperated.*"

How does a four-year-old even know that word and how to correctly apply it?

If I felt these emotions in the face of such a minor setback—one small reminder that I have little control over the world—it would seem that God must live in a constant state of exasperation.

My German friend Martin Schleske, a world-class violin craftsman, puts it this way: "Scriptures show me that God has the heart of an artist, not a grim construction planner. If the world were the work of a cosmic engineer, he would be in a constant state of discontentedness. We would all suffer from the constant nagging of a dogged designer whose plans just never work out like he intended or expected. Reality could never live up to his spotless construction plans. But a true Creator knows he not only has to shape, but also endorse and allow. Wisdom allows things to grow and unfold."

The sovereignty of God is not about deterministic control. So how does God reign? By being who God is: love and relationship.

Kim and I may be sovereign in our home, but once

the first child was born, any sense of control was out the window. If anyone was in charge, it was this new baby. He dictated everything—when we slept, when we woke, our state of mind, and how often we could visit with friends. Six pounds of humanity reduced a grown man to a weepy mush, ready to forgo usual and taken-for-granted pleasures, like sleep, in order to serve. It made us crazy, and it was sometimes incredibly hard, but we loved it, enough to do it five more times.

Love and relationship trump control every time. Forced love is no love at all.

I don't believe that the word *control,* in the sense of deterministic power, is part of God's vocabulary. We invented the idea as part of our need to dominate and maintain the myth of certainty. There is no sense of control in the relationship among the Father, Son, and Holy Spirit. When God chose to create humans—a high order of being who could say "no"—we were created inside the same love and relationship that has always existed. Control does not originate in God, but submission does. Domination does not find its source in God, but other-centered, self-giving love does. As our children's choices affect our relationship with them, so too do our choices affect our relationship with God. God submits rather than controls and joins us in the resulting mess of relationship, to participate in co-creating the possibility of life, even in the face of death.

4

"God does not submit."

I was sitting with my friend Andrew at a conference listening to an excellent exchange between Christians and Muslims, Israelis and Palestinians—you get the picture, people who almost by categorical imperative are required to be antagonistic to each other. But this particular gathering was different; the focus was on how the spirit of Jesus might cross all boundaries—ethnic, racial, political, etc.—and call us to something greater and grander than our divisions and disputes.

There is a common appeal, whether in the New Testament, the Hebrew Scriptures, the Koran, the Bhagavad Gita, the Analects of Confucius, etc., to what many of us would recognize as the Golden Rule. It is present in all of scripture and wisdom literature. Jesus stated it this way: "In everything you do, treat people the way you want them to treat you" (Matthew 7:12).

I leaned over to Andrew and whispered, "Do you think the Golden Rule applies to God?"

It was a simple question but with profound implications. Does God treat others the way God wants to be treated? If God communicated this same truth through so many messengers, it must first apply to God. But we often think that God gives commandments as if they are arbitrary tests for us humans rather than expressions of God's own nature. And if God's nature is love then ours is, too, because we are created in the image of God. Any command to love is to call us to *incarnate* the deepest truth of our being, love.

The Golden Rule is immensely significant because it is the way God is. God treats me exactly the way God wants to be treated. I don't have to earn God's love or love God first. And other people don't have to earn my love or love me first. I love because I was first loved (see 1 John 4:19). And the way I know *how* to love others is by asking myself how I would want to be disciplined, or have boundaries established in my life, or have my children cared for, or be forgiven and encouraged.

A central and inherent aspect of this other-centered love is the dynamic dance of mutual submission. It is how real life is lived and experienced, and it originates in the very being of God. *Submission* can be a beautiful word of relationship or a terrifying word of power and control. God is relational and therefore submits because God's nature is other-centered and self-giving love. One of the many beautiful aspects of the Trinity is that submission has always been within the very being of the Triune God, person-to-person-to-person, face-to-face-to-face. Theirs is a divine dance of mutuality in which no Person is diminished or absorbed. It is true submission, in which the Other is known and respected.

The very idea that God is submissive may be difficult for some folks, and may even sound disparaging—as if we're dragging our Holy God down to the level of human beings. But how often in my life has God whispered, "Let Me do this one because you make so many dumb choices. I think it would be better for us all if I

take over"? Never, right? Even though I would often pre-
fer that God make my decisions for me, God refuses.
Instead, God submits to the decisions I make, climbs

> *God is opposed to
> anything that is not of
> Love's kind, but God is
> always "for" us in the
> middle of the messes.*

into them, and begins to craft
something living and useful
and good, even from the worst
of my ignorant blunders—
even from my overt choices to
hurt and harm. Love doesn't
protect me from the consequence of my choices, but it

also does not abandon me to them. Nor does God's presence in the midst of our stupidity justify any of it. God is
opposed to anything that is not of Love's kind, but God
is always "for" us in the middle of the mess.

What if submitting, not in the sense of a doormat
type of false humility, but respectful and substantial
engagement between persons, is where authentic power
and authority originate? What is the incarnation—God
becoming fully human—if not complete and utter submission to us? What about the cross, in which God submits to our anger, rage, and wrath? Who but God would

take a towel in a room full of male ego and agenda, bow down in front of each man, wash his stinky feet, and gently remove the dust of the day to reveal the beauty of what was created to walk on Holy Ground?

I know a man who daily, hourly, minute-by-minute submits to his wife. He submits to her frailty and illness without any sense of being burdened or restricted. They are both in their eighties, but he is more physically able and so he submits to laundry, to preparing meals, to cleaning dishes, and to washing floors and toilets. He submits to her need to simply have someone present, and she submits to his care. This dance of submission has been learned over a lifetime. Only as we stumble toward wholeness does our capacity and ability to submit grow and increase and finally become as natural as it was intended. It is a call from within, sponsored by the Holy Spirit, to something greater and grander than power and control. It is a call to be truly human.

A year ago, this man who submits told me in a phone conversation that he deeply loves the woman to whom he is married, that she in many ways has saved his life, and that his greatest joy is serving her. I had never in my life heard such words spoken by this man, and it was almost as shocking as it was revealing. This man is my father, and the woman about whom he was confessing his love, my mother.

5

"God is a Christian."

*T*he *Shack* was not written for the world to read. I wrote it as a Christmas gift for our six children, most of it penned in longhand on yellow legal pads while I rode the metro to one of my three jobs. When I printed it on the photocopier at Office Depot, complete with spiral binding and plastic cover, I was thrilled. Giving those copies to my family and a few friends did everything I ever wanted or imagined that book would do. Not once did it cross my mind to publish.

I wrote the novel at the request of my wife, Kim. She'd asked, "Would you someday please write something as a gift for our kids that puts in one place how you think? Because, you know, you think outside the box." She was referring to my lifelong struggle with conflicts between faith and religion, and to my work both theologically and personally as I searched for helpful ways to think about God and humanity. Later, after I delivered the Christmas present, she told me that she had been thinking four to six pages. Oh well!

Obviously, the book has become something much bigger than what I'd originally intended for a small audience. As of this writing, *The Shack* has sold around 20 million copies. For me, this whole adventure has been a God-thing, but not everyone views it this way. While that book offered alternative ways of thinking about God and humanity that resonated intensely with many, it also challenged deeply held assumptions and embedded paradigms. For some, this was not a God-thing or even a good thing. Occasionally, precious people took issue with the imagery and concepts. I understand their concerns about my writing and, even more, am aware of many of the reasons such apprehension exists.

There is the infamous page 184 (depending on your edition), which has been a topic of passionate

conversation on many occasions. In the course of an ex-
change with the main character, Mackenzie, Jesus says,
"Who said anything about being a Christian? I'm not a
Christian."

Allow me to give you some background for this
statement. The term *Christian* was originally an insult
directed at the followers of Jesus, years after the resurrection. It basically meant "little-Christs" or "mini-
Messiahs" and was intended to demean the ragtag,
ragamuffin members of "that Jesus's Way cult." You can
imagine the litany of accusations brought against them
by people who thought they were dangerous, both to the
empire and to the religions of the day.

*"Who do you think you are? You live your life without
any real allegiances—not to Rome, not to politics, not
to Moses; and you waste your time caring for the poor,
the slave, the prisoner. Your relationships matter more
to you than your country or culture. You are all about
this* turning-the-other-cheek *and* going-the-extra-mile
*nonsense—both impractical ways of living, with naïve
commitments to other-centered, self-giving love. That will
never work in this world. Sure, you don't return evil with*

evil, you work hard, and tell the truth; but we can't count on you to keep our systems going. You are just a bunch of idealistic losers who are under the delusion that death can be defeated and who think the world could possibly be changed by love: little-Christs, that is all you are."

The idea that God is not a Christian is quite disconcerting to those of us who subtly if not overtly assume that our religious, human-defined "Christian way" is the best way and the way others should follow. Please hear me out: God is not a Muslim, either, or a Buddhist, an atheist, an animist, or any other category that we humans have manufactured in order to confiscate God and God's "blessings" over to our side of the ledger.

Why do we do this? Why must we insist on creating ways to define ourselves in opposition to someone else? Why do we then build empires based on these divisions, justifying our superiority and our brutality? We act as if our empires are condoned and supported by God.

The Scripture states that all things were created in and through and by Jesus, and it emphasizes that not one single thing has come into existence *apart* from Jesus. But our religions assume separation—being *apart*—

so when we hear the word *Christian,* we think of someone who started on the outside but then prayed a prayer
or did something special that moved him or her from
outside to inside. However, as the creator and redeemer
and sustainer of all things
(and this includes every single
human being), Jesus chal-
lenges every religious category.
If we take Jesus seriously,
then we are not dealing with

*Why do we insist on
creating ways to define
ourselves in opposition
to someone else?*

outsiders and insiders; we are dealing with those who
are seeing and those who are not seeing, trusting and not
trusting.

So is God a Christian? If you are asking if God is
about separation and treats people of different denomi-
nations, faiths, and ways of thinking as outsiders until
they pray a special prayer to "get in" . . . then, of course
not. If you are asking, does God relate to all of us as
beloved insiders who are completely ignorant and miserable, does God love us and incessantly find ways to lead
us to discover Jesus as our only way, truth, and life . . .
then, of course.

The New Testament was originally written in common Greek—Koine Greek (most of it). Guess what the Greek word for *accuse* is, as in "the Satan is an accuser"? (see Revelation 12:10). It is *kategoro,* from which we get the English word *categorize.* It means to put something or someone into a group to categorize them. We do this all the time, not always improperly, either. But when such categorizations carry an implicit judgment of value and worth, we are joining the adversary of our humanity, the Satan. Entering into divisive accusation reduces if not disintegrates the unity of our common humanity, and we become butchers of the Body of Christ.

Categories might be helpful in aiding our understanding and navigation through this cosmos in which we all dwell, but categories are powerfully divisive and destructive to relationships. For a child to learn the difference between *me* and *you,* parent and nonparent, safe and not safe, is good, but categories meant to establish healthy boundaries often turn into walls that frame prisons both for the "other" who are outside and the "we" who are inside.

If we all lived isolated in caves and were free to create all the boxes we wanted, that would be fine—no harm, no foul. But we don't. We live in community, and while many of us battle against an entitled, moral sense of cultural and religious superiority, we still have a tendency to cram everything into tidy mentally and verbally crafted boxes.

Believing (trusting) is an activity, not a category. The truth is that every human being is somewhere on the journey between belief and unbelief; even so, we perpetuate the categories of believer and unbeliever.

I am regularly asked if I am a Christian. My usual response is, "Would you please tell me what you think one is, and I will tell you if I am one of those." If the previous "little-Christ" description is how people today defined *Christian,* I would wholeheartedly accept and embrace such a categorization, and I would do it as a member of all the struggling communities of Jesus followers whether in the first or the twenty-first century. It is of utmost honor to be an expression of Christ and His life into the cosmos, to be that sort of Christian.

In *The Mystery of Christ—and Why We Don't Get It*, Robert F. Capon writes:

> *Christianity is not a religion. Christianity is the proclamation of the end of religion, not of a new religion, or even of the best of all religions. If the cross is the sign of anything, it's the sign that God has gone out of the religion business and solved all of the world's problems without requiring a single human being to do a single religious thing. What the cross is actually a sign of is the fact that religion can't do a thing about the world's problems—that it never did work and it never will.*

Christianity is not "the way." Jesus is the Way!

6

"God wants to use me."

Words mean a lot to me. They always have. Through words we exert presence, power, and creative force. But for all their potential beauty and empowering wonder, words also maim and destroy, tearing down as often as they build up. Like our eyes, our words are windows into our souls. Often, they reveal more than we intend. Our words tell on us.

I have never been a large man. I have lost every physical fight I have ever engaged in, and so I learned early how to war in other ways—with words. Hiding knives inside words, I could cut a much larger man to shreds and reduce him to bloody bits and pieces. Those wounds were often inflicted intentionally, hurting people deeper than any fist to the face.

But sometimes we allow mindless words to slide from our tongues—thoughtless words we use to cover our long-assumed presumptions. In some respects, these unconscious expressions are the most dangerous use of words.

I respect words. With two simple words God created light—"God said *light be*," and there was light (see Genesis 1:3). The entire cosmos was created by "the" Word (John 1:3). I also defend words, guarding their sanctity while exposing the ways they become weapons or controllers or false teachers. Words build up and even more easily dismantle and destroy.

It was my first time on a cruise. We left port in Miami and made a three-day swing down to Cozumel, Mexico, and back. Kim is not a big fan of water, especially when land is not visible, so I took Scott, one of my best friends, with me. It was a work trip. I had been invited to be one of the speakers on a music cruise, filling in the space between performances by various bands and musical artists. Scott and I listened to a wide variety of music genres, had adventures in the ports of call, and enjoyed many conversations as we made new connections.

One young man, in particular, became a friend. He is not a musician but a performance artist, and onstage he creates in-the-moment paintings that are raw and brilliant. He came and listened to me talk, and then Scott and I went to watch him create. Later, in the middle of a private conversation, our new friend said to us, "I just want to be a tool used by God."

Many well-meaning folks have said to me, "You are being used by God to touch so many lives." I do understand the sentiment and complimentary intent, but the words themselves reveal a misunderstanding of the character of God. That statement is more about a utilitarian god than the God of relationship, love, and respect so many of us have come to know in Jesus.

The dictionary says that a tool is "a device or implement used or worked by hand or machine to perform a task . . . something that helps to gain an end."

So I asked my new artist friend, "Would you explain to me how your relationship with your tools works? What does it look like? Do you confide your hopes and aspirations to your canvas or tell your brushes your secrets? Do they give you advice or mostly just listen?"

He looked at me, confused. "What are you talking about?" he asked. "I don't have a relationship with my tools."

"Exactly!"

To make the point more forceful, I explained that for people who come from sexual-abuse history, the last thing in the world we want is to be "used" by anyone, even by God!

> *If God uses us, then we are nothing but objects or commodities to God. Even in our human relationships, we know this is wrong.*

God is a relational being; that is who God *is*. The language of God is about partnering, co-creating, and participating; it's about an invitation to dance and play and work and grow.

If God uses us, then we are nothing but objects or commodities to God. Even in our human relationships, we know this is wrong.

Would any of us ever say to our son or daughter, "I can't wait for you to grow up so that I can *use* you. You will be Daddy's tool to bring glory to me"?

The thought is abhorrent when we think of those words in relationship to our own children, so why do we ascribe that language to God and how God relates to us? Have we so soon forgotten that we are God's children, not tools? That God loves us and would never use us as inanimate objects? That God is about inviting our participation in the dance of love and purpose?

God is a God of relationship and never acts independently. We are God's children made in God's image! God does not heal us so that we can be used. God heals us because God loves us, and even as we stumble toward wholeness, God invites us to participate and play.

7

"God is more he than she."

My book *The Shack* surprised a lot of people, and not all pleasantly. Some, like my own mother, were completely put off by my portrayal of God the Father as a large black woman called Papa. My mum did try to read the book. After all, one of her sons had written it, and people like her hairdresser and doctor were telling her about it. She made it to the point in the story where Papa came through the door, but once she realized what I had done, she closed the book, picked up the phone, and called my sister. "Debbie, your brother is a heretic!" She was serious and she was stuck.

Let me tell you the story of how my mum got unstuck and why she now loves *The Shack*.

In 1946, the pantheon of Western gods included Father, Son, Holy Spirit . . . and doctors. Doctors—almost exclusively male—dressed appropriately in holy, white attire and maintained a presence of aloof superiority and power. If a doctor stepped onto the sidewalk, everyone would step off until he passed. If a doctor walked into a chart room, everyone stood until he was finished and left. You never countermanded a doctor, especially if you were in training to be a nurse.

My mother entered a three-year nurses' training program at Royal Jubilee Hospital in Victoria, British Columbia, Canada, in 1946. She was eighteen, single, and wanted to eventually become a medical missionary. Three months into her training, shortly after she received her cap (which she said made her look cool, even though she still didn't know anything), a woman came into the hospital, bleeding. It was Mrs. Munn, the wife of Reverend Munn, the senior pastor of the Anglican church in Victoria. Medical records indicated that she had already lost five babies in late second and early third trimesters, and now her sixth pregnancy was in jeopardy.

It's difficult to lose a baby at any stage of pregnancy, but for those of you who have carried and lost a baby well after you can feel him or her kick and move, you know what a devastating road this is. Hopes and dreams had disintegrated for this woman and her husband, not once but five times. Now they stood on the edge of a sixth.

A doctor rushed in, examined Mrs. Munn, and said, "We are going to have to take the baby." An emergency C-section was hurriedly set up; and the doctor called the head nurse to assist and a student nurse to assist, learn, and do the cleanup. That student was my mum. Three months into nurse's training, this eighteen-year-old girl was thrust into the middle of an emergency C-section in which the doctor delivered a one-pound baby boy. In 1946 premature babies rarely survived, especially boys. There was no neonatal unit or NICU. State-of-the-art technology at that time was basically chicken incubators, boxes with heat lamps. And this baby was only one pound.

For a reference point, our third grandchild was born premature at four pounds and one-half ounce. I have a photo of his entire fist, with room to spare, inside my son's wedding band. The doctor placed Mrs. Munn's tiny, one-pound newborn into a kidney tray, handed it to my mother, and said, "It's not viable. Dispose of it," and turned to complete the operation.

My mother looked at the tiny baby, and he was still breathing. Disposal meant incinerator, where all medical waste was destroyed. She was caught in a monumental dilemma. In the service area outside the operating room, she found a washcloth. She wrapped the baby inside it, placed him in the kidney tray, walked back into the OR, and placed the tray on top of the sterilization unit, the only warm place in the room.

The doctor finished the surgery and, assuming everything was in order, left. The head nurse rolled Mrs. Munn to postop for recovery, leaving my mother to do the cleanup. This little baby boy was delivered at 8:30 p.m. on May 30, 1946. By 9:30 my mother had finished the cleanup and was sitting in a chair holding him, waiting for him to die. She thought that once the baby died, she would obey the doctor, and no one would have to be the wiser. At 9:30 the doctor met with the parents and gave them the terrible news; their son, not viable, had not survived. He left them to grieve the loss of their sixth child.

At 1:30 a.m. my mother decided she had better tell someone and called the head nurse who had assisted. "We are in so much trouble" was the response. The doctor was called and rushed in from home; he was furious. He ripped into this young girl, who because of her insubordination and inability to follow protocol had now put the hospital and him in the middle of a "situation."

"You created this problem"—he waved his finger at her—"so it is now your responsibility. But don't you dare say anything to the parents." Not knowing what else to do, this distraught nurse in training took the baby to the hospital nursery, where she and other nurses held him around the clock, feeding him with an eyedropper. Over the next two days, he lost four ounces.

Two days. What was the doctor thinking? Of course he was thinking that this baby would die, and once that happened, the entire "situation" would be swept under the rug of the code of silence.

And then this determined little baby began to pick up weight. The doctor realized that he had to tell the parents. "We did not want to give you any false hope. When your son was born, we were certain he would not survive, but . . . due to the miracles of modern medicine, we have managed to keep him alive, although chances are almost none that he will make it; and even if he does, there are certain to be complications, brain damage . . ."

They didn't care, not in that moment. They had a son, whom they soon named Harold (meaning good news). Later that day, Reverend Munn, holding his tiny infant son in one hand, baptized him with an eyedropper. No one expected little Harold to survive. But two weeks later, Mrs. Munn went home, and two months later, little Harold went home to his parents, and two years later, the nurses, including my mother, received an invitation to his second birthday party. My mother went, curious about Harold, and there he was . . . running and playing with the other children and looking perfectly normal. "A little skinny," she says now, recalling the moment.

She said nothing to the parents about how little Harold survived. She graduated, moved to central Canada, and entered Bible school, where she met my dad. They got married. Nine months later, I was born in northern Alberta, and ten months after that, the three of us moved to the other side of the world and the wilds of New Guinea, where I grew up.

Years later, we were back in Canada. I graduated from high school in northern British Columbia, in a town called Terrace. My mum was working at the hospital and happened across an Anglican newsletter, with an obituary for Bishop Munn. Curious, she asked an Anglican nurse she worked with if she knew the bishop. Turns out, the woman had worked with him, especially with First Nations peoples, and knew him well.

"Did he ever have any children?" My mother was still uncertain.

"Yes, one son, Harold. But I have lost track of him. Remarkable boy. Last I heard, he was a missionary teacher in West Africa."

My mother said nothing for another ten years and only then because she happened across another obituary—this one about the doctor who had given her such grief. It was only then that my mother told us, her family, about Harold Munn. She had kept this to herself all these years, but now that the doctor was dead, so too was the code of silence. She determined to track down Harold and tell him the truth about his birth. And she found him, now the senior pastor of the Anglican church just down the street from where his own father had pastored in 1946.

For six months she stewed, trying to figure out how to tell Harold "without him thinking I was looking for credit." Finally, she wrote him a letter at Christmas, wrapping his story inside another "coming of a Son story," the story of Jesus. Harold soon responded, and shortly after that they met. My mother told him the truth about his miraculous birth.

As you can imagine, my mother and Harold became quite close. One day, in a conversation, she said, "Harold, I have this son. He wrote a book, and I am having a hard time with it."

"Bernice, why don't I read it, and I will tell you what I think."

Harold read *The Shack,* and sent me an email. *"Dear Paul, I read your book. I love everything about it, but I think I know what your mum is struggling with: the imagery you use for God the Father. Let me see if I can do something about it."*

He blind-copied me on an email to my mother. *"Dear Bernice, I read Paul's book and you need to know I love it, but I imagine you are struggling with his portrayal of God the Father. Let me tell you why what he has written is so important to me."*

And he did.

As Harold pointed out, do any of us truly think that God is more masculine, more male, more paternal than feminine, female, and maternal? All of maternity, as all of paternity, originates in the very nature of God. The image of God in us (*imago dei*) is not less feminine than masculine. The feminine/masculine nature of God is a circle of relationship, a spectrum, not a polarity.

> *Imagery was never intended to define God; rather, imagery is a window through which we see aspects and facets of the nature and character of God.*

73

And imagery? It is all over the Scriptures: masculine (Father, King, etc.), feminine (Nursing Mother, Woman and Coin, etc.), animal (Mother Bear, Eagle, Lioness, etc.), inanimate objects (Rock, Fortress, Strong Tower, Mountain, Shield, etc.).

Imagery was never intended to define God; rather, imagery is a window through which we see aspects and facets of the nature and character of God.

Is God more masculine than feminine? Absolutely not! In my story about Harold Munn, who better represents the heart and character of God: the male doctor or the eighteen-year-old, single woman in nurses' training?

And finally, here is the wonder of this little story inside a story. My mother saved a one-pound baby boy in 1946 who decades later built the bridge that she could walk across toward her own son.

8

"God wants to be a priority."

Sometimes we relate to God as if magic were involved. We wouldn't call it that, but that's how we think it works. If I have the right formula (blood of a newt, eye of a toad) and the right words (*abracadabra* or *shazam*), I will get the right result (love potion number 9).

The goal is control, or at least certainty. If we pray the right prayer, we can get God off the throne and doing something—whatever it is that we think we need or want. Our formula could be *works* (do enough of the right activities, such as prayer, giving, reading the Bible, etc.), or it could be *faith* (if I have enough and exercise it properly, then . . .). Whatever it is, if we perform the formula, we believe that God will come through.

I didn't grow up in a family that had much in the way of material things—certainly not excess—but we always had the necessities: food, shelter, clothes. My father is from the generation who, even if they were not skilled in parenting, did duty well. I got my work ethic from both my parents, but especially from my dad.

Unbeknownst to me, my folks had put aside a little money to help me with my first year of college. But shortly before I left home, they invested it with a "trustworthy" religious man, and within a few months their savings and my college fund were nonexistent. I remember my mother, with tears streaming down her face, explaining what had happened. The look of utter bewilderment on her face was mixed with the emotions of loss and disappointment. "How could this have happened?" she said. "We tithed faithfully our entire lives!"

Magic. And when it doesn't work, we believe there is something wrong with us, with our formula. We didn't pray hard enough or long enough, or we didn't have enough faith, or there is some sin in our lives that has disconnected us from God.

The Greek and Aramaic vocabulary of the New Testament is tiny compared to English, and that of Hebrew (of the Old Testament) is smaller still, so translators employ many words that the original languages do not. Commonplace words from our culture have become the language of our spirituality, even though they are not in Scripture.

I have a massive set of Kittel's *Theological Dictionary of the New Testament,* a ten-volume collection containing thousands of pages of scholarly exploration of all the Greek words in the New Testament. When I want to understand how a word is being used, both within the context of the Scripture as well as its history and cultural framing, this is where I go. Volume 10 is the index for the other nine, and in it there is a Greek word for *principality,* followed by a word for *prison.* There are at least two significant words that one would assume should be in between those two but are absent: *principle* and *priority.* These English words don't have a Greek or a Hebrew counterpart. They are not in the Bible.

But these words are powerful in the business world and have been so embraced by religious vocabulary that we argue about who had them first. When have you heard a preacher who doesn't use the word *principle* or *priority*? Not often. These words have become part of the way we see and think about our relationship to life and to God, but they are not in the language of Scripture.

Jesus occasionally found himself in tricky conversations. The teachers and lawyers who asked him questions frequently had hidden agendas. Often they were men tasked with the preservation of the existing religious system and their own job security.

On one specific occasion, the question posed to Jesus was "Which of the commandments is the most important?"

This sounds like a question about priorities. Give me a list, Jesus. Rank the choices of my life in order of most to least important.

I must confess that religious people love this sort of list. I certainly did. It gave me a basis for self-righteousness and an external adjudication system that

"God wants to be a priority."

validated my effort and performance, especially in com-
parison to someone else. But there is a massive problem:
life doesn't work according to lists, and relationships
mess with any system of priorities.

What does it even mean to put God first? Is it a
percentage thing regarding our time or money or focus?
Surely, if we give God only part of our Saturday or Sun-
day, how is that making God a priority? Who decides
how much should be given in order for God to be a priority? How much is enough? Are there certain spiritual
practices, like prayer or church attendance, that qualify
in making "God first"? Who decides? And what happens
when I have a sick child who requires that I care for her
seven days a week, twenty-four hours a day? What about
my work? I sleep a good percentage of my life, so is sleep
exempt from the calculations? How do I juggle the list?
God first, family second, work or church, third? Hmm-
mmm!

I do understand that in accomplishing a task, it is
helpful to have a sequence of activity—do this first,
do this second, and so on. But our intentions can be
completely interrupted by a phone call, and suddenly

our agendas become irrelevant. I believe much of the frustration of our lives happens because our plans and expectations are interrupted.

So how did Jesus answer the question that seemed to be asking about priorities? He said, "The *greatest* and *foremost*"—remember those two words—"is to love the Lord your God with all your heart, soul, mind and strength." God first, right? God as priority.

Not so fast. Jesus then says, "The second is like it [the first]." How? The second is also "*greatest* and *foremost* . . . love your neighbor as yourself" (Matthew 22:36–40 NASB).

Instead of a list of priorities, Jesus introduced us to something completely different: a moving, dynamic, living relationship in which God is not *first,* but *central.* This is not a flowchart, but rather a mobile where everything is moving and changing as our choices and participation are woven inside the activity of the Holy Spirit. Lists are about control and performance; God is about adventure and trust. If God is at the center of our lives, then so is love and relationship, since God is profoundly both.

God doesn't want to be first on your *list,* but rather central to *everything.* This is not about pulling your mental catalog of priorities out of your purse or pocket and checking to see if what you have done is right or enough. This is about living in a relationship where plans might go

> *God doesn't want to be first on your list, but central to everything.*

completely awry, schedules can be massively altered in an instant, and we slip out of one season and into the next as quickly as a tide turns.

Moving away from the legalism of priorities and its inevitable guilt, especially in relationship to God, has opened up a huge space in my life and changed something fundamental in how I live. The reason I pay attention to my spouse is not because she is on my list, or to my family because it is a duty to perform, but because I love them and am in relationship with them, and they are important and significant. How that looks changes daily. The interplay of work, family, recreation, personal health, friendship, etc., constantly shifts and changes— a focus for a season here and then there. Instead of worrying about priority or balance, I get to live a life in which God is central to all of it and in which the wind of the Holy Spirit blows the elements of the mobile in unexpected and unanticipated directions, all the while inviting our participation in the moment, in the day.

9

"God is a magician."

I think most religious people would disagree with this statement. It is not a *lie* we believe. In fact, we would blush a little at the thought of *magic* being in the same conversation as *God*. However, I too have often related to God in precisely the same way that others use magic; I simply justified it with sanctified lingo.

By magic, I am not referring to card tricks and staged illusions, or even the mystery of art and music. The magic to which I refer in this essay is the means through which we exert control over someone or something. It is a power play that doesn't depend on relationship, which is messy and full of true mystery. It is the use of rituals, symbols, actions, gestures, and language with the aim of exploiting power. Behind religious magic is belief in a God who needs to be coerced to do something. The interaction is transactional. If I do the right thing or say the right prayer or incantation, then God is obligated to respond a certain way.

But I don't believe that God's response to our requests is ever because we performed the "right" actions or said the "right" words. God might act in spite of our expectations for "magic," but God's response is motivated by love, not by our performance or skill in prayer.

We religious people rely on two common kinds of magic—largely because we neither trust God's goodness nor God's love. How could God love us and want good for us, with all our sin, limitations, and blindness? The first kind of magic involves *faith,* and the second is based on *performance.* Either way, believing in magic makes us vulnerable to both outright charlatans and well-intentioned people who think they know the tricks of the trade. And when the magic doesn't work, we are filled with crushing disappointment and self-recrimination. After all, it can't be God's fault, so I must be doing something wrong.

With the first kind of magic, *faith*-magic, you should be able to move mountains, raise the dead, perform miracles, get rich, or have a baby. Then if something goes wrong, for example you get sick or a business fails, you either didn't have enough faith or you didn't exercise it properly. Or perhaps there is sin in your life that is impeding the flow of God's provision.

Let me state that I have no doubt that God is completely able to heal someone and raise the dead. I have personally seen the former, and friends I trust have witnessed the latter. In a sense, physical healing is simple: it's merely biological reformation that pushes the pause button on eventual physical death. But the healing of a human soul and reformation of heart and mind? Now that is a true and lasting miracle!

I married into a huge family, North Dakota/Minnesota salt-of-the-earth people. These folks don't do anything quietly. They are exuberant and love life. They argue, air their dirty laundry, are quick to forgive, and don't hold grudges. And most everything they do is loud, don't ya know! Basically, they are emotionally healthy. I, on the other hand, grew up in a rigid, religious family. We hid everything, lied about most stuff, and when we got together we had to have an order of service.

Early in our marriage, Kim and I went through an intensely difficult six months. Our firstborn was a little over a year old when my youngest brother, at eighteen, was killed in a horrible accident. Six months later, my niece was killed the day after her fifth birthday. Right in the middle of these two shocking losses, Kim's mother went into the hospital for fairly routine gallbladder surgery. She had diabetes, but hadn't taken care of herself. It flared up on the operating table, and within hours she was on life support.

Kim's family gathered together at the hospital to wait and grieve. I was in my detached, take-charge mode—dealing with the doctors and making phone calls—when the head doctor signaled that he wanted to talk to Kim and me. We were told that the family needed to make a decision. There was no brain-wave activity, so our choice was to keep her on a ventilator or remove her from the machines.

We walked back into the waiting room to deliver the news, only to find that the boyfriend of one of Kim's sisters was talking to the family, a number of whom were not Jesus followers.

"If you only had enough faith, your mother wouldn't be in there dying," he said.

"Wait," I interrupted. "Can you explain to me how this works? Are you saying that if the majority of us have enough faith, then she won't die?"

He nodded.

Then I asked, "What if one person has enough faith, will she live?"

He thought for a moment and then nodded again.

"Good!" I stated. "You're the one. If she dies, it's your fault!"

That was a rotten thing to say, I admit. But I was so angry. I would like to take a moment and apologize to so many who have been hurt by Christians who have been deeply unkind and insensitive because we had an implicit belief in magic, rather than in a God who joins us to be present and comforting in the midst of loss and suffering.

The second kind of magic, *performance*-magic, works like this: if I do the right things (read my Bible, attend church, tithe, pray, and go on mission trips) and if I don't do the wrong things (this list depends on the group you are part of), then God will bless me, and the things I pray for will happen.

As I boarded a flight from Asheville, North Carolina, to Atlanta—total airtime twenty-three minutes—I got a "nudge," which is one of the ways God talks to me, and I pulled out my last copy of *The Shack* before putting my bag in the overhead compartment. When the woman four people ahead of me stopped at my row, I let her know I was on the window, so she kindly put her bags down and waited for me to enter first. As I did, I tripped over the handle of her purse and sprawled into the seat, ending up with the book right in her face. Apologizing, I settled in, putting the book into the seat-back pocket.

She settled in, too, and then said, "You're not actually going to read that book, are you?"

Now it was on. "Actually, I've read it. Have you?"

"Yes, a year ago, and I didn't like it!"

"God is a magician."

"Really? What didn't you like?"

It was as if I opened up a machine-gun nest. A stream of generalities came my way, so fast and furious that it was hard to keep up. Something about violating the principles of God, not liking the portrayal of the Trinity . . .

"Wait, what didn't you like about the Trinity?"

She paused. "I don't remember," she said, and she was off to the races again, but this time the comments were more personal. When she paused to inhale, I asked another question.

"Do you know the author?"

She thought a second before answering. "Uh, no . . . but. . ." Have you ever seen the cartoon with the little lightbulb that flickers above someone's head? She had one of those. "Uh, you aren't the author, are you?"

"Yup!"

"No, you aren't!" She kept insisting that I wasn't until I showed her two credit cards and my driver's license. "This is such a God thing," she said as she leaned back and looked to the heavens. I wondered what she meant by that.

"Tell you what," I said. "Forget about the book. Instead, why don't you tell me your story? I am curious how you ended up on a flight sitting next to me."

So she shared her story with me. A year before, she was borderline suicidal. An addiction had owned her world, and she had lost every relationship that mattered to her. And then, thankfully, because of a group of street preaching fundamentalists, she met Jesus, and her life had turned completely around. But she was desperately afraid that she might lose the magic, might do the wrong thing or believe the wrong thing. Anything outside the principles she'd been taught was potentially dangerous. *The Shack* was dangerous.

> *She was desperately afraid that she might lose the magic, might do the wrong thing or believe the wrong thing.*

We began our descent, and I leaned over to her. "I am so excited for you! I have been walking this road with Jesus for a lot of years, and you are on the most incredible adventure a human being can have. I hope you never lose your fervor and focus. But, if I may, if Jesus were sitting here right next to you, I think I know what he would tell you."

"What?"

I put my hand on her shoulder. "I think he would say, 'relax.'"

Tears started rolling down her face, and I watched her melt into the embrace of an invisible but relentless affection. We hugged goodbye.

She smiled. "I'll try and read it again."

"It is truly okay if you don't," I assured her.

Twenty minutes later, on the train to my next gate and in the hubbub that is the Atlanta airport, I ran into her.

"Paul!" she yelled. She came over and gave me a huge hug. You would have thought we were long-lost friends. We were!

The alternative to magic is relationship, which is full of mystery and the loss of control. Magic is about knowing the right incantations, formulas, and performances. Relationship is about trust.

Do you know that God knows your language? Do you know you have the ability to talk to God and hear the voice of God, in your own unique way of hearing? You do. As much as magic might give us the illusion and promise of control, relationship is where the real action is, one moment at a time, a conversation of participation.

Once you taste the delight of relationship, you will never want to go back to magic again.

10

"God is a prude."

In the religious environment of my childhood, to say the word *sex* was to commit a sin. Meanwhile, the tribal culture in which I was raised (West Papua) was dramatically sexual. Many of the standard greetings were an association between sexuality and intimacy—the deeper the sense of relationship with another person, the more graphic the greeting.

Where do you think sexuality originates?

It originates in the very being of God.

Speaking of sex, members of the tribal cultures in which I was raised wore little if any clothing. There was no need. This was disconcerting for Western missionaries and, later, for the government who annexed the island. The solution? To airdrop tons of clothing into the jungle. But it is difficult to maintain a proper sense of decorum and respect when a chief comes prancing into the compound sporting a new "helmet" he found out in the jungle, complete with chinstrap. Personally, I would never have thought of using a bra as a helmet, would you?

Both sexuality and humor are inherently and profoundly relational. Both are capable of great beauty and creativity and of crass objectification and damage. With all the consternation, confusion, and havoc that human sexuality has caused, it must be incredibly significant.

Sex, money, and power: three great arenas of human interaction that if not continuously embraced by love become despotic and abusive. Of the three, only sex is an expression of being, something that is intrinsically an expression of self. But when any of these drift away from relationship, they become weapons of mass interpersonal and intracultural destruction.

The language of sexuality frames the scriptures of every religious tradition, including Hebrew and Christian. There is a celebration of the drive toward union, toward co-creativity, toward knowing and being known. When the New Testament tells us that the divine nature of God has been placed within us, the Greek word used is *sperma*. Sexual union is "knowing" another, the intimacy of face-to-face oneness.

As the early Christian church struggled to find adequate words to help describe the nature of God as Three Persons in complete Oneness, they landed on *perichoresis*, which means *mutual* interpenetration without loss of any individual Person. This is one of the best descriptions of sexual union I've heard, and it celebrates that this attraction and drive exist because we are created in the image and likeness of God.

This point is critical. Sexuality is a beautiful and creative force *only* when it is an expression of *agape*, a Greek word that means other-centered, self-giving, committed love. God *is agape* (1 John). At some point we severed sexuality from *agape* and legitimized the category of *eros* and its derivative, *erotic(a)*. In the classical world, Eros was a demonic god focused only on self-centered and self-servicing power in which the others were a means to the end of self-gratification (think pornography) and a fulfillment of the yearning toward wholeness (think infatuation). True love finds its fulfillment in the other and is, therefore, never blind. Infatuation is purposefully blind, finding its fulfillment only in the self and self-need. So it shouldn't be surprising that the word *eros* does not appear in Scripture, and when it appears in theological conversation, it stands in opposition to *agape*.

Pornography (like infatuation) is obviously nonrelational; it is an imaginary relationship that requires none of the risks of a real one. In fact, it is the opposite of *knowing*. Sexual objectification of women, men, or children in any sense is a turning away from love.

Romance, the joy of getting to know and care for the other, is a true expression of *agape*. Sexual intimacy, this iconic and stunning expression of our *imago dei*, is grounded in Scripture and is also an expression of *agape*, God's kind of love—other-centered and self-giving. When sexuality becomes self-centered self-gratification that uses the body or image of another as a means to an end, it is a devastating violation of love.

"God is a prude."

What if we begin to center all conversation about love and sexuality on *agape* as the wellspring and the beingness of all relational authenticity and respect? What if we reject *eros* as false, as the objectification of the other for the erotic encounter in which the self is served? What if *agape* is the ground of all authentic face-to-face intimacy, sexual and otherwise, and is a celebration of the flow of other-centered, self-giving love? Then knowing and being known make sense, and the depths of authentic relationship become essential to sexual expression.

> *When sexuality becomes self-centered self-gratification that uses the body or image of another as a means to an end, it is a devastating violation of love.*

The self-givingness of *agape* in no way denies the gift of the sensual, for this, too, is the celebration of *agape*. Self-giving *agape* is inherently respectful of the other, with no intention to diminish or absorb; it's mutual interpenetration without the loss of individual personhood (*perichoresis*).

I started by telling you about the tribe in which I grew up, where greetings were often graphic and sexual in their expression. Decades later, when the indigenous church was formed and healthy, a Western missionary raised the issue of language with the leadership. He was offended by the sexual overtones of their greetings. Graciously, they told him that they would have a meeting to talk about his concerns and would report back. When they met next, here is what the elders told the missionary: "When you are around, we will do our best and not use those words, but we are not going to stop praying that way." For them, human sexuality is a good and right language of intimacy. Turns out that it is not God who is the prude; it is us.

11

"God blesses my politics."

I have a confession to make. This is not the sort of confession that stems from secrets and lies and hidden things; I've already confessed all that stuff. You see, after thirty-plus years as a legal green-card resident alien, I have become a dual citizen—of both Canada and the United States.

Granted, I was a good candidate. I am a Canadian, and we all know that Canadians haven't caused much trouble for a long time; even the hint of such draws from us all manner of apologies. We would rather rely on humor than guns anyway. I have no ties to the Nazis or communists or any terrorist organizations, have never committed a felony, and have paid my taxes for decades. As a naturalized citizen I can never run for president, which I perceive as a benefit for everyone.

What I really want to talk about here is a different kind of dual citizenship—a dangerous mix of patriotism and religion. Generally speaking, patriotic fundamentalists are much scarier than religious fundamentalists, but the most frightening are those who are both. We must stop confusing nationalism and patriotism with the kingdom of God. We must stop trying to transform Jesus, the suffering servant, into the "Christ" of any political system, especially Western colonialist imperialism. And even though we might never be so brash as to declare that God is American, we Americans continue to act as if that were true. To be clear, I am not discounting that good people enter politics for good reasons and that even political machinery can accomplish good. There are many wonderful and good things about the United States and Canada, but beneath the thin layer of civility and civilization of every nation lurks a beast.

It has been an age-old presumption to establish

deities as local and geographic, with territorial agendas of special treatment for the chosen and conquest of the outsider—all in the "name of God." We have even seen biblical prophecy as justification for our existence and actions. Are we not the "city set on a hill"?

Maturing as human beings sometimes means realizing that our version of god was actually a local deity, largely fashioned by our own needs to control or manage an uncertain world. Sadly, this philosophy has often given us permission to justify and vindicate violence done in word and deed, and then to rewrite history through the lens of the victor and oppressor.

Even more grievous is that many men and women have sacrificed life and limb to protect local, political deities. These good people have suffered the casualties of war as they tried to help the oppressed, the victimized, and the abused.

God is not an American. But neither is God Serbian nor French nor of any other human-erected and empowered political or social identity. Since we were all created in God's image, would it seem more correct to say that God has worked through many of our political avatars in order to protect our people and cultures, while working with us to destroy everything that is false?

Political identities do not originate in God. God is not about separation and division, not about building walls and excluding, not about domination and power. These all find their source in our chosen darkness, largely fueled by greed, fear, and the drive to establish security and certainty. Let's face it. We are afraid! And since trusting God only seems helpful in the long term (eternity), we rely on and give our allegiance to something we think is more tangible, more immediate, and that presents itself as powerful enough to protect us and give us what we want. We give our fidelity and loyalty to an obviously broken, humanly originated system rather than risk trusting an invisible God.

It doesn't take much to reveal that politics is not a solution. New Guinea, the land I grew up in as a child, has more than eight hundred unrelated language groups. Tribes, separated by rivers, mountains, and swamps, have completely different dialects. This is an anthropologist's dreamworld but a political nightmare. One of the first attempts to "civilize" the tribal communities was to introduce a two-party system. They split the tribes by giving half umbrellas and the other half sweet potatoes. It worked great until the first rainfall, when the umbrellas failed miserably. Everyone then joined the sweet-potato party and consumed the entirety of their political divisiveness.

While humorous, this also reveals an unrelenting tension that exists between the kingdom of God, which has *no* political alliances or agenda, and the kingdoms of this world (which are always founded in bloodshed). Left-wing policies express the same blindness and lust for power and control as do right-wing policies. If we are so bold as to identify ourselves with the kingdom of God, which is supposed to be an *alternative* to the kingdoms of this world, then everything about what we do and why we do it must change, including all of our allegiances.

Government is not instituted by or originated by God. We built it. If you want to find the roots of political power, look no further than to the book of Genesis and to Cain, who murdered his own brother. Cain turned his face completely away from God and left to follow an independent and destructive destiny. He established the first city and named it New Beginnings (Enoch), after his own

firstborn son, and he built an empire. Within five generations, Lamech was wielding ruthless political power, taking women as property, and giving his own daughters
names that reduced them to
objects of physical attraction.
Humanity was off to the races,
competing for territory and
power regardless of the costs.

> *Only a kingdom that changes us from within will deal with the fear and hate that expresses itself in nationalism and patriotism.*

Every nation-state on the
planet exists because of the
bloodshed of brothers. Every
human being bears the *imago
dei*, the image of God. What is birthed out of murder
cannot be ultimately justified, no matter the hymns and
praises written to its glory.

The only option to the insanity of political empire is
the kingdom of God. Only a kingdom that changes us
from within will deal with the fear and hate that con-
tinues to express itself in nationalism and patriotism.
We are afraid. We don't need new powers to defend
and protect and divide and conquer. We need healing.
Peaceful resistance then becomes the path that changes

the world without becoming absorbed by the systems. Everything costs. It will cost us to engage a violent world from within a borderless kingdom that is other-centered and self-giving. Look at what our commitment to self-centered greed, self-righteous superiority, and territorial fear has already cost us.

If you ever see my immigration folder, there is a note in it. William Paul Young will not kill anyone on behalf of this country. Nor would I for any country. A gun is an immediate response to a perceived threat, but the impact of violence is devastating for generations. Thankfully, we belong to a kingdom in which violence is never an expression of allegiance. If you think that "turning the other cheek" is the coward's way out, may I wager you have never tried it.

12

"God created (my) religion."

A man arriving at the proverbial Pearly Gates is unsure what to do. *Do I simply walk in?* he wonders. St. Peter, who seems to always be on duty in these stories, recognizes the look of consternation on the man's face, approaches, and asks him if he might need some guidance.

"I'm not sure what I am supposed to do," the man begins. "Do I simply walk in?"

"It depends," says Peter, smiling.

"It depends?" The man is surprised. "On what?"

"It depends on how many points you've earned," offers Peter.

"Points? I need points? How many points do I need?"

"A hundred."

A hundred? the man thinks to himself. *That can't be difficult, surely I have earned a hundred points.* He turns back to Peter. "So, for the last fifteen years I have been serving on Saturday nights at the soup kitchen, helping with the poor?" He offers it hopefully, more a question than a statement.

"That's wonderful!" exclaims Peter. "I will give you a point for that."

"One point?" The man is shocked and looks at Peter, who is enthusiastically nodding. In that moment the man realizes that this is not going to be easy.

"Well," he hesitates, "I was a pastor for thirty-five years. I did everything that was asked of me. Preached and married people, counseled and buried people . . . ?"

Peter is looking grim, "Ah, I don't know . . ."

"Peter, please, thirty-five years."

Peter thinks quietly for a moment and then smiles. "Okay, I will give you a point for that!"

Now the man knows he is in trouble. His whole life had been basically summed up in two points and he has ninety-eight to go.

"God created (my) religion."

Movement catches his eye, and looking across the way he sees a man who had lived in the same town in which he pastored. He didn't know him well; he was the sort of person who came to church services on Easter and Christmas. He did remember that this man owned or worked at a coffee shop in town and had always seemed pleasant, but he'd never engaged much with the religious community. To his surprise, the man smiles, waves, and then without hesitation walks right in through the Pearly Gates.

"What?" he exclaims, turning to Peter. "Are you telling me that that guy has a hundred points?"

Peter laughs, "Oh no, he just doesn't play this game."

I love this joke—not only because it catches us by surprise, but because we quickly feel its sting of truth. Many of us try to win the affection and approval of God by our behavior, and so it seems that behavior and performance are deeply woven into most religions.

But God did not start religion. Rather, religion is among a whole host of things that God did not *originate* but *submits* to because we human beings have brought them to the table. God is about relationship;

and therefore, any understanding of church or any community of faith that is centered on structures, systems, divisions, and agendas has its origin in human beings and not in God.

"Religion," by definition, is *people*-based, not *God*-based. Here's how the dictionary, in part, defines religion: "people's beliefs and opinions concerning the existence, nature, and worship of a deity or deities . . . an institutionalized or personal system of beliefs and practices relating to the divine" (Encarta Dictionary).

> *Religion is among a whole host of things that God did not originate but submits to because we human beings have brought them to the table.*

Human beings form religions around the things that matter to them and the fears that drive them toward certainty. For many, Christianity has become a religion.

Jesus is not the founder of any religion. He did not come to start a new religion to compete with the myriad of other religions that already existed. Rather, Jesus indwelt an inclusive family of faith—in which we are learning to celebrate the presence of God (contemplation and action) and the presence of each other (community).

Now, let me say this: just because human beings come up with organized ways of doing things doesn't make those systems inherently evil. Religion is a construct, a way of doing things that almost always embodies both beneficial and destructive elements— destructive when they disconnect from relationship and love. Like all human institutions and organizations, religion often becomes a means to control something or someone or other human beings, and this applies to the Christian religion, too.

The word *religion* derives from two Latin words, the prefix *re-* meaning "back" or "again" and *-ligio,* referring to "something that binds one thing to another." Religion is my attempt to bind myself back to God—a noble gesture, but one doomed from the start and quite impossible. What began as a relationship with a living Jesus often devolves into a religion, defined by what we do: external activities, posing, right words, clothes, holy gestures, hushed tones. We forgot that Jesus is in us and that we are invited to participate in His promptings, ideas, and viewpoints, learning to actively take sides with Him against the way we see God, ourselves, others, and creation.

If we will look to Jesus rather than religion, we'll be delighted to find that as religion falls away, so too will the sacred/secular filter that has been our lens. We will realize that our fatherhood, motherhood, friendship, ditch digging, garbage collecting, gardening, bread baking, coffee brewing, whale saving, weed killing, caring for our neighbor, and bird-watching are all expressions of participation in the life of God.

Back to *The Shack* and another bit that got me in hot water. Jesus is about to go into his workshop, and Mackenzie stops him with a question: "Do all roads lead to Papa [God the Father]?"

"Not at all." Jesus smiled as he reached for the door handle to the shop. "Most roads don't lead anywhere. [But] I will travel any road to find you."

While religion might be an impediment to us, it is not to God. Religion cannot be an end in itself or else it will become despotic and harmful and will inevitably traffic in human souls in order to maintain its own existence. Every institution—political, social, or religious— must answer to something or someone. For me, the measure by which to judge any human institution, as well as my own life, is the person of Jesus.

Rather than being led by Jesus, however, human beings routinely become controlled by the very systems and institutions they create, often belying original intentions for greater freedom and good. What was originally intended to promote human well-being too often becomes a system of incarceration.

The Jewish system had some wonderful practices. One of these was the internal reset button, the Year of Jubilee. Every fiftieth year, they would push this button and everything went back to zero: debts, liabilities, punishments, etc.; the whole system was supposed to start over after a year of celebrating our common humanity. By the way, that reset button was God's idea, for our benefit.

I wonder what the planet would look like if we applied this Jewish experience to our world. In addition to the Year of Jubilee, the Jews were also required to give the land a Sabbath every seven years. Every seventh year, they were not to plant or harvest anything from their fields—but to allow the land to rest (see Leviticus 25). What if, after each six years, we all took a Sabbath year to think mindfully about what we are doing and how better to participate in exercising compassionate dominion together, and then every fiftieth year forgave all debts, for all nations and individuals—all debts? Why not? The way we are doing things now is not working very well.

What if in our faith families we gave ourselves a time-out to celebrate the presence of God and the presence of each other?

13

"You need to get saved."

One of my many jobs over the years was in sales. Although I was fairly successful at it, I didn't like doing it. Even when I sold insurance, I focused on commercial lines of coverage; it felt better to sell to a corporation than to an actual human being.

What bothered me most about selling was treating people like targets. Every conversation was a potential sale, every contact a prospective network. Yes, sales make the world go round, but the love of money can lead to all manner of evil (see 1 Timothy 6:10).

Some of my closest friends are excellent sales-people. They are people of high integrity and are gifted relationally, but the line between authentic serving and usury is a fine one that concerns them deeply. Remember those invitations at church for a Friday night get-together that turned out to be an unwanted sales pitch? After your first foray into the world of multilevel marketing, is it any wonder that it was hard to accept an invitation to coffee? Worse, if you were bitten by the multilevel bug, it was only a matter of time before you were bereft of friends— even family crossed the street when they saw you coming.

It's about the transaction, signing the dotted line. I pay you this in order to get that. It could be a new car or a sense of security or sex or entry into heaven.

How can we not see that bad religion is no different? How is it not a multilevel sales pitch that treats people like targets?

Perhaps you get an invitation from a friend. You go. A product is described. Maybe it is Jesus or a way to ease your loneliness or a promise of life after death. Then there is a transaction, a signing on the dotted line. In much of Christianity it is "saying the sinner's prayer." Now we are in someone's downline, and they get a reward for facilitating our salvation.

After you "sign," you are informed of the "fine print" in the contract. There is a proliferation of expectations that no one told you about—minimum performance standards, time and money commitments, and innumerable rules. If you behave right and meet performance objectives, you could become a district manager and eventually reach the Star Level. And if you don't . . . well, we don't want to talk about that, do we? Okay, since you brought it up . . . If you don't follow through on your commitment, you will be in danger of being eternally tormented in a lake of fire, and if you don't get the ones you love in your downline, they will, too.

Wow! Why would I ever think this is great news?

Should we be surprised that people are leaving the brick-and-mortar sales meetings in droves? Or that young people who are already oversold in the market don't want to be sold a relationship with God?

So what is the Good News? What is the Gospel?

The Good News is *not* that Jesus has opened up the possibility of salvation and you have been invited to receive Jesus into your life. The Gospel is that Jesus has already included you into His life, into His relationship with God the Father, and into His anointing in the Holy Spirit. The Good News is that Jesus did this without your vote, and whether you believe it or not won't make it any less or more true.

What or who saves me? Either God did in Jesus, or I save myself. If, in any way, I participate in the completed act of salvation accomplished in Jesus, then my part is what actually saves me. Saving faith is not our faith, but the faith of Jesus.

God does not wait for my choice and then "save me." God has acted decisively and universally for all humankind. Now our daily choice is to either grow and participate in *that* reality or continue to live in the blindness of our own independence.

> *God does not wait for my choice and then "save me." God has acted decisively and universally for all humankind.*

Are you suggesting that everyone is saved? That you believe in universal salvation?

That is exactly what I am saying!

This is real good news! It has been blowing people's minds for centuries now. So much so that we often overcomplicate it and get it wrong. Here's the truth: every person who has ever been conceived was included in the death, burial, resurrection, and ascension of Jesus. When Jesus was lifted up, God "dragged" all human beings to Himself (John 12:32). Jesus is the Savior of all humankind, especially believers (1 Timothy 4:10). Further, every single human being is in Christ (John 1:3), and Christ is in them, and Christ is in the Father (John 14:20). When Christ—the Creator in whom the cosmos was created—died, we all died. When Christ rose, we rose (2 Corinthians 5). At the back of this book, I have listed a chain of scriptures, *a catena,* that relates directly to this conversation. Please take time to read through them.

The context of salvation involves three dimensions. First, prior to the foundation of the world, we were all included; we were all saved in eternity (2 Timothy 1:9). Second, we were all included in the birth, life, death, resurrection, and ascension of Jesus (2 Corinthians 5:19). Third, within the context of our own present-tense, ongoing experience, we actively participate to *work out* what God has *worked in* (Philippians 2:12–13).

Although we didn't do anything in the accomplishment of our salvation (except to kill Jesus), our participation in the working out of this salvation is essential. Our ongoing choices matter.

But we must not let the cataclysmic, cosmos-reforming truth of what Jesus has "finished" be reduced to transaction and sales. Paul the Apostle writes, "From now on we no longer judge any person according to the flesh" (2 Corinthians 5:16). We don't judge anyone by how he or she is stuck or broken or lost, but see each person for who he or she is—the one the Holy Spirit finds and celebrates, the one Jesus leaves the ninety-nine to go find, the one the Father waits to welcome home. We don't offer anyone what has already been given; we simply celebrate the Good News with each one: *We have all been included.*

I recently held our newborn grandchild in my arms and wondered about the incredible creativity and purpose of God. This immortal being would not have come into existence without the participation of two human beings and God working in concert. For nine months, the lives of many adjusted in anticipation of this arrival.

"You need to get saved."

The ongoing life of this child will also be wrapped inside the participation of human beings. The working out of our salvation, fully secured from all eternity in Jesus, is also participatory. We don't participate in the working out in order to make it true; we do so because it is true.

14

"God doesn't care about what I'm passionate about."

Do you ever get asked about your hobbies? For a long time, the question stumped me, because I really don't have any. There are many things that I enjoy but have never become a focus. Perhaps I am too easily distracted. I have friends who have hobbies, like gardening, fishing, golfing, hiking, biking, blacksmithing, crafting fishing lures, making music . . . but not me. I participate in all of these with my friends, but I normally would not go out of my way to engage in these activities, and certainly not alone.

Recently, through the kindness of friends, I was able to surprise another of my golf-loving friends with a two-day visit to the Augusta National Golf Club in Georgia to watch practice rounds before the main event there this year. As we walked, he regaled me with stories: This is the fifteenth, where Gene Sarazen hit the "shot heard round the world," a double eagle in the last round to tie and force a playoff, which he won. And here on the sixteenth is where Tiger Woods made that chip, the ball hanging on the lip of the cup, boldly displaying the Nike symbol, before disappearing to the roar of the crowd. And Larry Mize's chip-in win in his playoff, and Bubba Watson hooking a shot through the trees and around the TV tower and gallery for a tap-in putt to win. And right here, this is the thirteenth hole, where Phil Mickelson—from two hundred yards—hit a four-iron around a massive pine tree directly in front of him and stuck it on the green less than ten feet from the hole.

For two days we walked and watched and talked, and I loved every minute of it. And then it struck me. I do have a hobby. It is to climb inside another person's passion and experience his or her joy. Once I realized this, I could see it everywhere in my life, with one child who loves physics and statistics, another who thrills at music and movies, a grandchild who draws or paints or dances, and another who terrifies with the breakneck speed of his three-wheeler. Then there's Kim, who loves mothering, grandmothering, and creating spaces of welcome; and friends who gift us with stories and photos of their own child, grandchild, or hobby.

Where does such delight originate?

A few years ago, my friend Baxter boarded a flight heading from Atlanta to Washington state. It was his first trip to the Pacific Northwest, and he chose a window seat at the back of the plane in hopes that he might catch a glimpse of the Rocky Mountains. The flight was only half-full, and no one was sitting next to him, so he settled in. Then a strange thing happened. The jet, which had already pushed away from the jet bridge, suddenly stopped and pulled back. The door opened to allow one more passenger to board. Curious, Baxter looked to see who this important person was, and what he saw almost made him laugh. The man looked like Indiana Jones stepping out of the jungle, complete with hat, high leather boots, a leather satchel across his chest, and five-day stubble on his face. The man passed all the empty seats and, smiling, settled in next to Baxter in the back row.

Now, Baxter is a southern how-you-and-your-mom-doing gentleman, and introducing himself asked, "So what do you do?"

"I am a systematic microevolutionary botanist," he said.

"Really?" Baxter paused. "May I ask what a systematic microevolutionary botanist is?"

"I find and rescue endangered plants." He went on to explain that he had just returned from a five-day exploration in Central America. Taking out a piece of paper, he began to draw plants, adding their scientific names and breaking down their properties. He made lists of flora that were extinct and those that are on the edge of disappearing. He explained the incredible properties these plants contained that would help human beings deal with pain and disease, and he made notes on the search for their seeds.

An hour into the conversation he stopped. "So Baxter, what do you do?"

"Well, I am a theologian."

"God doesn't care about what I'm passionate about."

The man paused. "I suppose you want to talk to me about evolution."

"Not really," Baxter replied. "I don't care much about that, but please, tell me more about plants."

Normally, Baxter only cares about plants if a bass might be hiding behind one, but he found himself caught up in this scientist's delight. Another hour of pictures and stories went by before Baxter said, "I do have a question for you. Where did your passion come from? I mean, were your parents scientists? Was Aunt Sallie-Mae a botanist?"

There was thoughtful silence for a couple of minutes while his new friend pondered the question. "No one has ever asked me that before. I don't know where my passion comes from. It sort of just . . ."

"Evolved?" both said at the same time, and laughed.

"If I may," offered Baxter, "I can tell you."

"You can tell me where my passion comes from?"

Baxter nodded, taking out a piece of paper and drawing three intertwined circles, representing the Trinity. "Look, this is the symbol for the Three-Person Oneness of God. Inside of this moving divine dance of relationship, everything was created: every human being, every plant, every subatomic particle, everything. God loves His creation and loves our participation in it. That passion you feel that moves you to care for creation? That is Three Persons of God sharing Their heart and love for the creation with you. And when you are hiking through the jungle in search of these plants, you are participating in the work of God."

That passion you feel that moves you to care for creation? That is Three Persons of God sharing Their heart and love for the creation with you.

The man sat stunned. "Why hasn't anyone ever told me this?"

Exactly! Our love for our children and our family and our friends originates and is embraced and enfolded in God. The farmer who plows the field participates with God in love by supplying food to celebrate the Bread of Life? The desire any of us has to explore and serve and work hard and create and draw and build and sow and dance and learn and grieve and cry and sing and imagine and wonder and fish and pray and golf . . . all these desires are expressions of the very nature of a God who celebrates our life and our humanity.

This God will never be cloistered inside walls but will join us right where we are. God never abandons or forsakes and is not content to let us stay inside brokenness or the lies we have believed. This is a God who is fully and utterly committed and engaged and loves to celebrate us and our passions. Your joy and your love and your grief and your fury and your hope and your curiosity and your drive toward authenticity and integrity and your wonder all originate in God.

What an amazing thought!

15

"Hell is separation from God."

I grew up in religious environments that were steeped in the dread and specter of eternal conscious torment. My deepest motivation for right living was not the reality of love or trusting in the life of Jesus; it was the fear of hellfire and damnation.

The topic of hell is a massive one, sparking all manner of heated debates. There are a number of basic views of hell, including 1) eternal damnation, 2) annihilation, and 3) an age of redemptive purification. If you would like to step back a moment and take another look at this particular conversation, let me recommend a good place to start: Brad Jersak's book *Her Gates Will Never Be Shut* (2009).

For many, the crux and conflict of the question is how we can posit an eternally Good God, whose very nature is Love, allowing human beings to be in conscious torment and pain for infinite time, as if that were somehow Just.

The thought is so disheartening that, for many, it becomes an insurmountable obstacle. I regularly receive emails that say, "I am terrified to take the risk and trust that God is as Good as you have written, and then find out you are wrong." Doesn't it seem intuitively wrong to be desperately afraid of a torture-devising God and yet hope to spend eternity with this God?

In *The Shack,* I tried to move the conversation about hell from the head to the heart by putting the main character, Mackenzie, in the crosshairs of a terrible dilemma. In the cave where Mack faces the Wisdom of God, Sophia, She demands that he take the position of Judge, a role that he, like all of us, assumes daily. But Sophia turns the tables unexpectedly.

"Choose two of your children to spend eternity in God's new heaven and new earth, but only two . . . and three of your children to spend eternity in hell."

"Hell is separation from God."

Sophia is driving the reality of this issue away from a disengaged, heady debate and down into the deepest recesses of the heart and soul—the visceral love of a parent for his or her children. It also exposes the lie that God is not a loving Father—not even as good a parent as we are—and the lie that this remarkable, unreasonable love we have for our children originates in us and not in God.

Sophia is unrelenting, and She begins to examine the behaviors and attitudes of Mack's children, and thereby reasons that he might justify his choice to send three of them to hell. In Her mock argument, judgment is assumed to be based on behavior and performance, the keeping of a record of their wrongs (an activity that 1 Corinthians 13 states emphatically that love does *not* do).

Driven into an abyss of hopelessness, Mackenzie finally sees that there is only one way out, a way that any mother or father, with even the smallest degree of health, would choose.

"Could I go instead? If you need someone to torture for eternity, I'll go in their place. Would that work? Could I do that?" He falls at her feet, crying and begging. "Please, let me go for my children . . . please."

Agreeing that the entire topic of hell is too massive for a simple chapter, I want to address one significant element: the belief that hell is separation from God, from Love, from Light, from Goodness.

Consider this simple line of reasoning. Either hell is a created place or thing or it is not. If it is not created, then it must by definition be God, who alone is uncreated. In this sense, hell would be God, who is a consuming fire. Your destiny would not be apart from God but directly into God, who is Love, Light, Goodness.

The other alternative is that hell is a created place or thing. Consider this passage: "For I am convinced that neither death, nor life, nor angels, nor principalities, nor things present, *nor things to come*, nor powers, nor height, nor depth, *nor any other created thing*, will be able to separate us from the love of God, which is in Christ Jesus our Lord" (Romans 8:38–39, emphasis added).

"Hell is separation from God."

This is a list of all the realities that *cannot* separate you from the love of God. What isn't in the list, keeping in mind that it includes "any created thing" or any "thing to come"?

Nothing. There is nothing absent from the list.

You are a "created thing," so therefore you do not have the power to separate yourself from the love of God. And whatever hell is, if it is a created thing, it cannot separate you from the love of God.

Please keep in mind, saying that we cannot ever be *separated* from the love of God is not the same thing as saying we cannot *reject or ignore* the love of God. What we choose to believe, even if a lie, becomes our experience. I have the power to choose to live in the blindness of assuming that I am separated from God. I may have convinced myself or been convinced by others that I deserve to be separated from God. Such lies will bring with them a shadow in which I experience a sense of separation, feelings that seem to validate the illusion that God is not connected and in

> *What we choose to believe, even if a lie, becomes our experience.*

relationship with me or that God has stopped loving me or has given up on me. Many of us on the planet live in this illusion *now*.

Consider with me: Anyone who speaks of separation from God assumes that a person can still exist while separated—as if our life is not contingent upon the presence of God, who is Life. Does that mean we have eternal existence apart from Jesus and the Father and the Holy Spirit? Scripture is emphatic: not one thing has come into being apart from Jesus, and the existence of everything is completely dependent upon the sustaining life of Jesus.

So, if we continue this thought . . . perhaps hell is hell not because of the absence of God, but because of the *presence* of God, the continuous and confrontational presence of fiery Love and Goodness and Freedom that intends to destroy every vestige of evil and darkness that prevents us from being fully free and fully alive. This is a fire of Love that now and forever is "for" us, not against us. Only if we posit that we have existence apart from Jesus can we believe that hell is a

"Hell is separation from God."

form of punishment that comes to us in our separation from Jesus. I propose the possibility that hell is not separation from Jesus but that it is the pain of resisting our salvation in Jesus while not being able to escape Him who is True Love.

16

"God is not good."

"God is Good, all the time! All the time, God is Good!"

It's a common greeting—"God is Good, all the time!" You will often hear it in gatherings of people of faith. We don't say this in order to make it true, trying to convince ourselves that God is worthy of our trust. We remind each other that, in spite of all circumstances, challenges, and losses, this is the truth. We say this to counteract the lie that constantly whispers to us that God is not Good. But even so, this lie creeps in. We question the goodness of God. Especially in the face of tragedy and loss, we might begin to believe that God is not Good.

A woman reached out to me recently via email. She's an incredible human being, a woman who lives in the constant agony of persistent physical pain. She's endured this pain for years, and she is exhausted from the war that rages within her own body. She's not suffering as a consequence of personal sin or failure. She just suffers. Not only is my friend fighting a battle within her own body, she also has a child who lives in chronic pain. And, as if that weren't enough, my friend has endured the loss and grief of relationships that have disintegrated in all the ripples. There are times when living in this world isn't fair or just or good.

> She's not suffering as a consequence of personal sin or failure. She just suffers.

And she is mad at certain Christian writers. "I finally *hated* reading Christian authors because they'd write from either head knowledge or the other side of their suffering." And then she asked me, "Would the books you've written look different if they had been written in the middle of increasing and debilitating pain that makes it hard to see or feel? I just want to know: If you were sitting in the pain right now, would you feel the same? Would you write the same? Why am I sitting here sobbing?"

Good questions. Questions that invited me to stop and listen. Go back, if you would, and reread what she said. Let yourself feel on her behalf—if not for your own losses. To lament is to be present.

Yes, God is able to heal, instantly and thoroughly, but even raising the dead is but the press of a pause button, a temporary reprieve from the event of death. Ask Lazarus. But miraculous and instant physical healing seems to be the exception, not the rule. For every person who stands up and testifies to the wonder-working power of God's miraculous healing, there are ten who wonder, why not me? Why did they not qualify, or what was so unworthy about them that they were passed over? For every miraculous escape, the visible hand of God, there are many who sob into their pillows because a child, spouse, parent, or friend wasn't rescued and didn't survive.

None of us is immune from suffering. I state that as an observation, not in any way to discount my friend's or anyone else's pain. We live in a world where there is great loss—whether consequences of our or others' sin or natural results of living in a broken world. We know this intellectually and, when we allow ourselves, we feel it.

I wrestled with this in my book *Eve*:

"Then why didn't God—why didn't God protect me?"

Eve let it hang there, suspended and ominous, the question uttered by a billion other voices. It rose from grave sites and empty chairs, from mosques and churches, from offices, prison cells, and alleys. Tattered faith and battered hearts lay broken in its wake. It demanded justice and begged for miracles that never came.

I first tried to address this in *The Shack*. In the movie version there is a scene that takes place the first morning after Mackenzie has returned to the shack. His night has been a turmoil of horrific dreaming, and he emerges the next morning onto the porch, disoriented and filled with controlled fury. Papa has already prepared breakfast and is waiting for him. He sits but doesn't touch his food while She talks.

Finally, She turns to him and says, "Mackenzie, the underlying flaw in your thinking is that you don't believe that I am Good. Until you believe that I am Good, you will never be able to trust me."

He spits out his response. "Why would I ever trust You? My daughter is dead!"

In my email conversation with my friend, this is how I responded.

The answer is, "of course" my books would look different. How different would depend on when and where you caught me in my own journey . . . there are times when my character might have ended locked in a mental institution or run away by suicide. One morning my writing might have glimmers of hope, but by that evening would reflect the chasms of despair.

While I am able to put myself back into those moments and times, it is not a place that lasted forever nor a place I would want to reside. By the end of The Shack, *Mack still has a ton of stuff to work out, and Missy is still murdered. Tony is dead by the end of* Cross Roads. *And Lilly? By the end of the novel* Eve, *her healing process is truly only beginning. But it is hope that remains the framing.*

You bring up a good point, though, and I will have to sit with it as I think about my work yet ahead. If I were in that pain, and if I were even able to write, I truly believe that I would write that pain. I think your anger at "Christian" writers, generally speaking, is justified. Too often everything gets resolved and all is well by the end of the story. Our lives are certainly not like that. But this world is not all there is, and death is not the definer or solution.

So, I live in this world, with a daughter who has fought a brain tumor almost ten years, another daughter struggling to reconcile a three-year damaging relationship, a son and daughter-in-law who are on the healing side of losing a baby well into pregnancy, a son still recovering from the sudden death of his best friend . . . and on, and on, and on. Perhaps we are incapacitated when lost in the midst of sorrow and pain until we forget we were created to fly.

But pain also has a way of making everything stark and real, and validates your questions. I am so sad with you about all your losses. I don't understand the mystery of what it means that you and I, as participants in this broken world, are "filling up the sufferings of Christ" [see Colossians 1:24]. But I do believe that our participation and presence in suffering brings meaning and a possibility of redemption, even if only within ourselves.

Your sobbing is the utterance of tears against the losses of our humanity. If I could, I would fix it. Gentle hugs on a very hard day!

The existence of evil is a wrenching question, but the greater philosophical/theological question is why any Good exists at all. God, who alone is the source of Good, is Light in Whom there is no darkness. If God is not Good all the time, then trust is delusion, and we are truly left alone in a world of hurt. Our pains and losses can blind us to the Good that surrounds us—the grace that is constantly poured out and the life and light that push away the illusion of darkness. Even in the midst of crushing tragedies, with their unanswerable questions and losses that seem about to sweep us away, there is a solid rock, a place to stand, a profound agreement and potent declaration of trust that we can make, even if it only feels like barely a toehold:

"God is Good, all the time! All the time, God is Good!"

17

"The Cross was God's idea."

Children have a wonderful capacity to ask exposing questions, largely because they haven't yet had their worldview hardened into assumptions. So they ask to know and not to show off how smart they are.

When our son and daughter-in-law were in Uganda working through the process of adopting and bringing Maisy home, their other children (our grandchildren) stayed with us. The oldest of the three was five at the time, and one day as we were driving in Grama's car, she asked a question.

"Hey, Gramps, when Maisy has been here for a while, will she turn white?"

"Nope."

"What?" she exclaimed. "Do you mean that she will always be brown?"

"Uh-huh," I responded.

There was silence from the backseat as the new information was being processed.

"Good!" she finally affirmed. "This family needs more brown babies."

It was that simple. Maisy was coming to make our family richer and more wonderful. But the conversation began with an exposing question, a question that by its asking is enough to challenge sleeping assumptions and open up possibilities that would otherwise remain dormant.

Here is another challenging question: Who originated the Cross?

We now come to the single, most profound and far-reaching events in the history of humanity (in my opinion): the life, death, resurrection, and ascension of Jesus. Without this sequence of events, faith as it relates to Jesus would be wishful thinking. But more specifically, I want to talk about the Cross, the instrument of torture that murdered this man who claimed to be God.

Let us be unequivocally clear: there is *nothing* good about a cross. It was devised as a torture machine to implement the most profound humiliation and abuse. Its purpose was solely to keep a human being alive as long as possible and in as much pain as possible until his very breath (spirit) was violently ripped from his body through excruciating suffocation. The point of eventually breaking the legs was to speed the process so that the executioners could go home to waiting meals and families.

Who originated the Cross?

If God did, then we worship a cosmic abuser, who in Divine Wisdom created a means to torture human beings in the most painful and abhorrent manner. Frankly, it is often this very cruel and monstrous god that the atheist refuses to acknowledge or grant credibility in any sense. And rightly so. Better no god at all, than this one.

The alternative is that the Cross originated with us human beings. This deviant device is the iconic manifestation of our blind commitment to darkness. It is our ultimate desecration of the goodness and loving intent of God to create, an intent that is focused on the human creation. It is the ultimate fist raised against God.

And how did God respond to this profound brokenness?

God submitted to it. God climbed willingly onto our torture device and met us at the deepest and darkest place of our diabolical imprisonment to our own lies, and by submitting once and for all, God destroyed its power. Jesus is God's best, given willingly and in opposition to our worst, the Cross.

> *Jesus is God's best, given willingly and in opposition to our worst, the Cross.*

When did God submit? Not only in Jesus incarnate but before the creation of the world, according to Scriptures (Revelation 13:8). God knew going into the activity of creation what the cost would be. That God's own children, this highest order of creation, would one day make the final attempt to kill Life.

And how would we religious people interpret this sacrifice? We would declare that it was God who killed

"The Cross was God's idea."

Jesus, slaughtering Him as a necessary appeasement for His bloodthirsty need for justice. Isaiah (in chapter 53) prophesied this: "Although he bore our sin and suffered at our hands, yet we considered him punished and afflicted and stricken by God . . . and in Jesus, God encountered/embraced [*paga* in Hebrew] our twisted rebellion and brokenness."

I made at least one significant mistake in *The Shack*. Most people wouldn't notice the little detail, but over the years since I wrote the story, I am more certain that it is, indeed, a mistake. If the screenwriters put this scene in the movie, I will have asked them to change it.

Mackenzie, the main character, has returned to the shack, a broken hovel of a place in the wilderness. This is the possible site of his daughter's death and the focal point of his great sadness. He goes here to confront either the perpetrator or the God of his Christian heritage who has remained distant and unapproachable and who did not protect the one he so deeply loved. The God of his assumptions does not show up, and Mack, in fury, destroys the place until his strength is gone. He screams his hate at God and declares himself to be finished.

As he leaves to return home, a transformation takes place, not within him but in his ability to see. The shack of his tragedy seems to be reformed into a habitable place; he hears the sound of laughter from within and hesitantly approaches the place of his devastation. As he raises a fist again, but this time to knock, the door flies open and Mack is face-to-face-to-face with three people he does not know.

Later, when Mackenzie reenters the shack, he looks to where his daughter's bloodstain should be, and it is gone.

Mistake!

It should still be there. Even when we work through our great sadness, our losses and betrayals, the evidence of what we have done or what was done to us does not disappear. Instead, it is worked into what we become. And while evil is never justified, it is redeemed and rescued from its intent, thus becoming a statement of true justice.

This is Jesus. God submitting to our torture machine and transforming it into an icon and monument of grace, so precious to us that we wear it on our rings or around our necks. This torture device declares that there is nothing I can bring to the table that is so evil or broken that God won't climb into it with me. There is nothing so dead that God is incapable of growing in it something living. The Cross, once our greatest attempt at destroying Life, has become our most precious symbol of the God who is hope for us all.

18

"That was just a coincidence."

Until children are taught otherwise, they believe they can speak the language of God. They are not determinists caught in a vise of evolutionary fate, nor are they believers in religious karma; rather they are participants in a free-form dance of mystery and adventure and relationship. They intuitively know the language of delight. If the adults who attend them stop and listen, they might be reintroduced to the world of wonder through the gasps of amazement and shrieks of surprise, which so easily spill from children onto anyone willing to be so brilliantly contaminated.

Those of us who have left our childlikeness behind

in order to become adults may have lost the art of their language. It is barely remembered or is blocked out. But God invites us to once more become like children, for in doing so, we will begin to see the wonders of the world with which we are surrounded—the kingdom of God. It is akin to the gift of entering into a foreign world, a culture that is unknown to you, and your first task is to learn its language. If you don't, please don't expect anyone there to comprehend what you attempt to communicate.

God has never lost the ability to speak "children." In his book *Orthodoxy*, G. K. Chesterton writes:

Because children have abounding vitality, because they are in spirit fierce and free, therefore they want things repeated and unchanged. They always say, "Do it again"; and the grown-up person does it again until he is nearly dead. For grown-up people are not strong enough to exult in monotony. But perhaps God is strong enough to exult in monotony. It is possible that God says every morning, "Do it again" to the sun; and every evening, "Do it again" to the moon. It may not be automatic necessity that makes all daisies alike; it may be that God makes every daisy separately, but has never got tired of making them. It may be that He has the eternal appetite of infancy; for we have sinned and grown old, and our Father is younger than we.

Childhood was God's idea, and theirs is a language of simple trust and delight, of fun and surprise, of comfort and tenderness. It is the language of the unexplainable and coincidence, where meaning is found in the confluence of disparate pieces of life that meld together to become a new surprise. As we become adults, God doesn't stop speaking "child" to us, because it remains our native tongue, even though we sometimes forget the words and lose touch with the joy of its wonder. Perhaps one of the reasons we adults enjoy attending animated movies with our children is that they that remind us of who we are.

God is an expert at language. In fact, the entire cosmos was created by a single Word. But rather than demanding that we understand God's language, God comes to us and speaks ours. Even more specifically, God speaks *yours*. You have a language that is unique to you, thoughts and words that make you smile on the inside or laugh when no one else does, or hurt and grieve when those around you don't. I sometimes think that we all expect to hear God speak to us in a language that belongs to someone else, and we discount the possibility that God knows ours. Ours is so common, so ordinary, so usual, that we trivialize it. But why would God, who comes to speak life to us, not speak in our own language?

Coincidence is firmly a part of the language of a child. When our children were growing up, we and a half-dozen other families would be visited by leprechauns, and for the week before St. Patrick's Day, these tiny pranksters stirred up all sorts of mischief and fun adventures—setting traps, turning milk green, tying all the shoes together, and creating a constant disarray of treats and treasure hunts before they headed back to Ireland. Part of the wonder is that the children would begin to find connections between events that the adults never orchestrated.

"That was just a coincidence."

I believe that God, who is Good all the time, is involved in the details of our lives, speaking to the child that is still alive within us, though at times deep in sleep. I believe that we are surrounded by the language of coincidence, usually so subtle that one would have to be present and paying attention to notice and hear, but at other times virtually undeniable as to its origin.

One of my mantras is "Coincidence Has a Name!" There are no chance encounters; detours are usually intended destinations that are simply not in *our* planner or agenda. Part of participation with the flow of the redeeming genius and creativity of the Spirit is to be present

> *Be present enough to pay attention to the glory and kind humor that surrounds us.*

enough to pay attention to the glory and kind humor that surrounds us, even in the midst of profound loss and agony.

Recently, I did a book signing at a mall in Johannesburg, South Africa, and I met Susanna. The manager had told me about her, about how many copies of *The Shack* she had bought and through them engaged her

159

ninth-grade students. Some of her students came from intensely difficult areas of the township of Soweto. Susanna is a steely wisp—a twentysomething who brims with a caring, compassionate determination, while light slips through her eyes and words as we share time and hugs.

She asked me to sign and write a note on two blank sheets of paper to two of her students—one who had days before attempted suicide and the other for that girl's closest friend. This closest friend had witnessed another girl succeed. Later I signed another page for her entire ninth-grade class. One of Susanna's students had witnessed her brother being killed on the streets, and all of them were working hard at healing the war-torn bits of their sense of worth that had been disintegrated by abuse and crushing circumstance.

A few people had gathered for the event, and it was time for me to speak. Earlier that day, I had been told that I would be doing a "reading" from *Eve,* the novel I was there to help launch in South Africa. In the last nine years of book signings and speaking events, I have only been asked to read from my own writing two or three times. It is not something I normally do. I borrowed my publicist Anje's copy and quickly scanned pages as we rode the Gautrain from Johannesburg to Pretoria. I dog-eared two sections as possibilities, and that evening as I opened *Eve* to read, I chose the latter, a conversation between Lilly, a broken fifteen-year-old girl, and Eve, the mother of all Creation.

It is a difficult passage but one that anyone who has experienced loss and tragedy would readily understand. At its heart was a simple yet profound question, "Why didn't God protect me?"

As I read, I started getting choked up, emotion unexpectedly rising to the surface, my pauses between phrases witness to the struggle I was having to keep my composure. I am always curious when this happens. I never know what is triggering something in me—the invisibles within or without. It was a short "reading" and I closed the book.

I then spent the next hour responding to questions, and after that another hour signing books. Susanna waited. As we finally sat together, she opened a copy of *Eve* to the section I had read. Her eyes were filled with tears.

"It is astounding to me," she said, as she looked at the pages open between us, "that you would choose this passage. Of anything in the entire book, you picked this."

I waited.

"You see," she continued, "what you don't know is that a few weeks ago one of my girls succeeding in killing herself. Since then there has been a domino effect, and six other girls have tried to do the same, including the girl you wrote the note to and the other who witnessed her best friend succeed. The method? They jumped off a building."

I was already crying, and now there weren't any words except those embedded in the tears and the hugs. The passage I had chosen randomly, by chance, coincidentally, on a whim, or whatever other term we use to distance ourselves from the always-present activity of the Spirit, contained these words of Lilly:

"I feel like I'm climbing a mountain that has no top. I'm barely holding on to the rock wall. I'm scared, and everyone expects me to make it. If I don't, it's like all that's wrong in the world is going to be my fault."

"That was just a coincidence."

Lilly leaned her face into the woman's neck and whispered, holding back emotions. "What if I can't do this and I let go? Or, what if I jump, will God still catch me?"

"He will, but to you it will feel as though you hit the ground."

Surrounded as we are, in the ordinary and extraordinary, inside the mundane and the unusual, in what so often appears to be random and exempt from purpose, I am personally convinced that nothing is apart from the abiding presence and activity of God. I trust that *coincidence* has a Name.

19

"God requires child sacrifice."

We live in a world where child sacrifice is, sadly, not uncommon.

A few months ago I was invited into a reunion of women and men representing decades of missions. As children, we had been sent to boarding schools and hostels because our parents were spreading the Gospel. Being raised this way was both a blessing and a curse for each of us; we all knew the joys of exposure to diverse cultures—but these joys were often entwined with the jolting losses of separation from family. Almost all of us had been sent away to boarding school by age six. To me, now, this seems unimaginable, but for us, then, it had been the expectation and the norm. It was part of our duty, the sacrifice we made so that others would hear about Jesus. Some of those at the reunion, each one precious, are so profoundly wounded that they would count the verbal references made to Jesus or God in a conversation or speech, and once the number reached six, they would get up and leave. It was simply too painful.

A Third Culture Kid or Missionary Kid (TCK or MK) grows up in a culture different from their parents'. Often we were pulled out of our childhood world and deposited back into our parents' home culture—a new and completely foreign place, with new customs and languages to learn and to which to adapt. We then returned to the "mission fields"—which were our first homes—and discovered the sadness that we no longer truly belonged anywhere.

I grew up in the highlands of West Papua, which covers the western half of the island of New Guinea, which sits just above Australia. West Papua was formerly known as Irian Jaya, and before that, Netherlands New Guinea. My parents, along with a one-year-old child (me), were Canadian pioneer missionaries to the "utter-most parts of the world."

Christian missions have a checkered past, accomplishing incredibly important and worthy objectives while also being a source of undeniable misery. It was often a two-edged sword, and nowhere did it cut more bluntly than in the lives of the missionary's own children, who were often sacrificed on the altar of spreading the Good News of the Gospel of Jesus. The good ends of salvation justified the means, and the presence of children was often viewed as an impediment to the mission; their losses were necessary costs for the "greater good."

About fifty of us were all sitting in a circle at the reunion when I asked the question: "How many of us struggled with and were punished and humiliated for bedwetting?" At least a third of us raised our hands, some of us in our sixties and seventies. Stories were shared of embarrassment and shame, often attended by nervous laughter barely holding back tears. This is only one of the costs of being a living sacrifice.

A few years ago, our son and daughter-in-law began the arduous process of adopting a little girl (Jael O.) from

Uganda. There are brutal beliefs in parts of the world, and two of these are that if you impregnate your own daughter it will protect her from evil spirits, and if you have sex with your child it will protect you from AIDS. This is an example where good intent and sincerity count for nothing. It is wrong and abusive. Jael O. is the child of incest, her mother and aunt both impregnated by their father. Jael's aunt died in childbirth at thirteen, but her mother survived Jael's birth at fifteen. Jael was unwanted, a throwaway child, and rescued as an infant from the streets by a kind Ugandan woman. She was a year and a half old when our own children entered Jael's life—traveling half the world to find her after a year of preparations and paperwork. The legal hurdles were substantial, and it took two months in the country before she was allowed to leave with her adoptive parents.

During those eight weeks, six little boys went missing in a one-mile radius of where Jael lived. Two appeared back on the streets, but the other four are presumed dead. For eighty U.S. dollars, you can pay someone to abduct a child who will be murdered and sacrificed to territorial spirits, their body parts cut up and buried in the corners of new construction and businesses as protection against financial failures. The two boys who survived had both been circumcised and therefore, we can only assume, were too "blemished" to be useful.

If we sacrifice our children on the altars of religion or nation-state or career advancement or job security or financial gain or scientific progress, should it surprise us that we attempt to justify our actions by "seeing" them in the very character of God? If it's good enough for God . . .

One of the narratives about God is that because of sin, God required child sacrifice to appease a sense of righteous indignation and the fury of holiness—Jesus being the ultimate child sacrifice. Well, if God is like that, then doesn't it make sense that we would follow in God's footsteps? But we know intuitively that such a thought is wrong, desperately wrong.

And herein lies one of the most damning impacts of religion (or patriotism or nationalism, etc.). It wields the power to justify its actions by grounding them in the purposes and will of God. The Scriptures themselves not only become the narrative for poor choices at best but also for the perpetration of horrendous abuse.

It is the undeniably overt declaration of Hebrew Scriptures that God hates child sacrifice and is opposed to it in any form. But one of the stories that *seem* to justify it is that of Abraham and the almost-sacrifice of his son Isaac. The larger context is a series of missteps on the part of Abraham, in which he tries to help God out of one predicament after another. And each time he "helps," disaster results, and with each misfortune, God submits to Abraham's choices

Religion wields the power to justify its actions by grounding them in the purposes and will of God.

and creatively works to build something good out of the rubble. Abraham has already put Ishmael out of the home, which greatly grieved both God and Abraham, but then God asks Abraham to put out Isaac as well, permanently. Abraham is broken. No more arguing as he did regarding his nephew Lot, no more lying as with King Abimelech, no more coming up with his own provision as an answer to the impossible. It seemed that this God might not be any different from all the others, after all.

The only religion that Abraham had known in Ur was appeasement; in fact, every god on the planet at that time required sacrifice in order to either pay for poor performance or to move the hand of a deity to act on one's behalf. Whether you were in Africa, South or Central America, Asia, or the Middle East, all gods were appeasement deities, and religion was largely a system of control by magic through sacrifice. The mythology of power through performance has devastated humanity from the beginning.

Read again the story of Abraham and Isaac. (It's in Genesis, chapter 22.) This is not a story about God requiring child sacrifice, but rather the opposite. The point of the story is that God will step into our darkness and speak our language in order to reveal something we didn't know: that this God does *not* require child sacrifice. Abraham "named the place The Lord Will Provide. And to this day it is said, 'On the mountain of the Lord it will be provided'" (Genesis 22:14). So if we, the human race, require a sacrifice, God will provide Himself.

Our granddaughter's name, Jael, is a strong name—meaning the one who ascends (mountain goat ibex). Our son and daughter-in-law gave their little girl a new first name, Jael remaining her middle name. Echoes of Isaac, the promised son, we call her Maisy, which means "longed-for child"!

20

"God is a divine Santa Claus."

Sometimes it takes a crisis or a crossroad for us to arrive at the place where we are able to let our old, faulty understanding of reality go and begin embracing a better and truer one.

Author and speaker Brian McLaren once stated something that goes like this: "Every authentic move toward God has to go through atheism." I think he means that as we move forward in our journey and relationship with God, we will discover that God is not who we thought. We may have to deny the faulty and flawed perceptions we once treasured in order to open ourselves up to the God we are growing to know.

Over the years I've met a number of people who have had trouble letting go of their childhood imaginations of Santa Claus. Not that they still believe in this fairy tale, of course; rather, they have projected their notions about Santa Claus into their thinking about God. Let me explain.

We all have misguided and often incoherent views of God, and the imagery of Santa Claus will help us look at some of them. I think there are two basic ways we tend to see God as Santa Claus: as the Nice Santa God and as the Nasty Santa God.

The Nice Santa God is wondrous, full of surprises and childlike fun, hiding gifts and enjoying our anticipation as the day approaches when we will finally open what is waiting for us. But even as we celebrate that Santa God, there is an unease.

In the 1930s, a Christmas song was written with a happy upbeat jingle that inadvertently unmasked the reason behind the angst.

He knows if you've been bad or good,
So be good for goodness' sake!

"God is a divine Santa Claus."

It's a threat. Of reward and judgment for behavior. You can't hide from Santa God. Even crying is poor performance, so you'd better not. Watch out! Santa God has a list, keeping a record of wrongs, even tabulating it twice to make sure who is "in" and who is "out." Santa God is watching your every move, even when you sleep. Santa God knows when you've been bad or good, so be good . . . why? (How is this for goodness' sake? The songwriter must have just needed a word that rhymed with *awake*.) The real reason is so that you get the reward for proper performance and are judged good, compared to the bad children who won't be getting anything this year. Another one of those subliminal suggestions that the poor, who have nothing, are bad.

The response I get from this Santa God depends wholly on my performance. Worse, if suffering and bad things are happening in my life, we know who is at fault. Me. And why? Because I must have been bad.

For many of us, the Nice Santa God is represented by Jesus: approachable, affable, a friend who always has our best interests at heart. The Nasty Santa God is our imagination of the darkness behind Jesus—God the Father. It is God the Father who requires perfect performance and moral behavior.

God the Father is not a different sort of Person from Jesus the Son.

If we behave properly, with righteous and holy decorum, we will ultimately be rewarded at the Grand Christmas Party in heaven. If not, and you were bad, well . . . it was a lot worse than not getting presents.

God does not struggle with dissociative identity disorder. God the Father is not a different sort of Person from Jesus the Son. God is not Santa Claus. Santa God is a projection of our own wounds and shame onto the face of God, as well as our wish that God might be the fulfillment of the deep hope and yearning that naturally resides in a child's heart.

Many of us were raised with childish notions about God, sometimes planted in the gardens of our souls by others who had the best of intentions. But those ideas have found root and become assumptions that continue to engage our minds and hearts without question. Don't be too surprised when the Holy Spirit begins messing with your garden and digging around in things that you might have long thought precious.

There is a scene like this in *The Shack*. Sarayu (the Holy Spirit) and Mackenzie are digging in the garden. Initially reluctant, Mack finally enters into the work without truly understanding its purpose or even that he is working in the garden of his own heart and soul. He responds to a compliment from Sarayu:

> *"I didn't do that much, really," he said apologetically. "I mean, look at this mess . . . and even though it seems like lots of work still needs to be done, I feel strangely at home and comfortable here."*

The unearthing of our treasured imaginations, bringing assumptions to the surface, can be painful and disorienting. It is hard work, but it is good work. As lies and false imaginations about God are exposed, so are the roots that are entwined in our thoughts about ourselves and about our neighbor. More work! Pulling weeds is arduous, but at the end of a day's work, it is rewarding, even if it is the simple joy of being a little more comfortable inside our own skin.

No one has a relationship with Santa Claus—not the nice one or the mean one. Santa Claus does not exist, and one cannot build any kind of relationship with an idea or construct. The Nice/Nasty Santa Claus is largely a projection of our shame or guilt or wishful thinking, or even the longings to be important, remembered, loved, and significant. He is an icon, a window, through which we look at ourselves; and sometimes in our misperceptions, we imagine we are looking at God.

To understand who God *really* is, you can begin by looking at yourself, since you are made in God's image. All the things you long to be true about who you are—authenticity, kindness, patience, integration, goodness, purity of heart—these are qualities of the God in whose image you were created. While these qualities may not be your experience, they are still your yearning and deepest desire. Even better, look at Jesus, the human being who is the incarnation of the character and nature

"God is a divine Santa Claus."

of God. As we begin to stumble toward the Light and Life of the goodness of God, our need for imaginary substitutes, like Santa Claus, will quickly fade. And we will discover that real life, even in its suffering, is much more deeply rewarding than imagined life.

21

"Death is more powerful than God."

A few months ago I was sitting with friends in a hotel restaurant when this book project came up. At this time in the process, I was exploring words that God would never say, and I was asked to give an example. The one I chose in the moment, though provocative, was also one that I had spent a great deal of time thinking about and working on, which is probably why it popped so readily to mind.

"God would never say, 'I'm sorry you died. There is nothing I can do for you now. Death wins.'"

Please keep in mind that I was talking with friends, good friends. They love me and my family. They have high regard for my novels, *The Shack, Cross Roads,* and *Eve*. They have heard me speak on multiple occasions and have been nothing but encouraging. They are engaged, thoughtful, and articulate.

"Paul, what do you mean?"

"I mean that I don't think God would ever say that once you die, your fate is sealed and there is nothing that God can do for you."

"But that's true!"

"What's true?" I asked, beginning to sense that the conversation was about to go in a completely unexpected direction. What was meant as a simple example was suddenly taking center stage.

"It's true that once you die, it's over. Your fate is sealed, your eternal destiny locked."

The intensity of the response indicated that I had entered waters that were considered sacred. My intention made no difference. I had stepped on a land mine. At this point, one of the friends at lunch declared, "Oh there's someone I need to talk to," and left before the tension increased.

Let me pause in the middle of this story to clarify a

couple of important things. There are certain ideas we assume are true because they haven't yet been challenged by life. For example, when we face a tragedy, we sometimes act as if the tragedy is bigger than God—even though we would state that we don't believe this to be true. We freak out over financial insecurity, while saying that God is trustworthy. We would state that God, who is Life, is bigger than death, but we're terrified in the face of death. It is also obviously true that I don't know everything and that dialogue is a gift to help work through ideas. We all get triggered—when assumptions seem to be at risk, when we begin to feel defensive, when an idea is disorienting, or for reasons that reside in our past or journey.

Back to my conversation. I thought I chose my next question carefully. "To be clear, you don't think we have any choice postmortem, after we die? You don't think we can change our minds?"

"Of course you can't! That is why you have to choose Jesus as your Lord and Savior during this life. Once you die, you can't change your mind."

I realized I had not tripped a simple land mine, I had inadvertently set off a cluster bomb. If I went in one direction, explosions would go off elsewhere. What was I to do? I looked for a question that might help us focus. It wasn't helpful.

"Is it possible that the intent of judgment is to help us clear away the lies that are keeping us from making a clear choice?"

"Are you saying you don't believe in hell?"

"Let me ask you this: Do you think that love and relationship are possible without choice? I think that coerced love is no love at all, and love without the ability to say no is impossible. Don't you agree?"

"Yes, but you have to make that choice while you are alive!"

"But that means that love and relationship end with death. It means that death defines everything."

"You can't choose after you die. You can regret the choices you made, but you can't change it."

"So what if I never knew I had a choice or didn't live long enough to make a choice? What if I had mental illness, and my mind was fragmented? What if I died in the womb?"

"There is special grace for such people."

"Then why didn't God strike me with mental illness so that I could get special grace?"

At this point my friend burst into tears.

"Why are you crying?" I asked.

"Because I think this is really dangerous. I am worried for you."

"Is it possible that the intent of judgment is to help us clear away the lies that are keeping us from making a clear choice?"

You see, my friend loves me. Truly loves me. Since what I was proposing could not possibly be right, I was potentially a danger, not only to myself but to many others as well. You may feel the same way.

Life is filled with the need for these kinds of conversations, as difficult as they feel in the moment. Iron does sharpen iron, but as my friend Jerry always said, ". . . if the angle is right." So even as I presented my point of view to my friend who disagreed, or present it to you in this chapter, I want the angle to be right.

Personally, I do believe that the idea that we lose our ability to choose at the event of physical death is a significant lie and needs to be exposed; its implications are myriad and far-reaching. I am not proposing that life and death are equally opposing forces. Death is nothing compared to Life; in fact, it is the absence of Life. God is Life and Light and Love; God is not death or darkness or fear or bondage. I am suggesting that love and relationship are possible only when we have the ability to choose.

I think evil exists because of our turning from face-to-face-to-face relationship with God, and because we chose to say no to God, to Life and Light and Truth and Good. God, with utmost respect and reverence, submits to our choice even while utterly opposing it. God, who is Love, not only allows our choice but joins us in our humanity in order to rescue us from our choices that are harmful and destructive. God has gone to incredible lengths to protect our ability to say no, even though that freedom has produced unspeakable pain and loss.

If God (who is Life) has gone to such great lengths to protect our ability to say no, why would we think that the event of death would have the power to take away our ability to say yes?

Or to put it another way: If our ability to choose is the reason for all the devastation in the cosmos, and if that freedom is taken away postmortem, then why didn't God simply take it away to begin with? God could have prevented all this terrible tragedy.

I propose that the event of death introduces a crisis (*krisis*—the Greek word, as in "Day of . . . *judgment*"), a restorative process intended to free us to run into the arms of Love.

I believe that children and the mentally ill will be the first to recognize Love as who God is and will dance into the Relentless Embrace of Eternal Affection. I think the devastated and the damaged, the discarded and abused will also more readily choose the God of Love than we who are religious. The stories of Jesus clearly reveal that the religiously inclined have always been the greatest challenge; but even for us, Life is bigger than death.

22

_____

"God is not involved in my suffering."

As a high school student, Maggie was returning from an early morning run when she got separated from her cross-country team. She was abducted by a man, dragged behind a building, and raped twice. Then she was strangled, buried under brush, uncovered, and shot five times with a .22-caliber pistol—and left for dead.

In an email to me, Maggie wrote that she . . .

. . . knows exactly what it feels like to have the peace of Christ in you when absolute hell is happening to and around you. Though I didn't understand where it was coming from at the time, I'll *never forget the "calmness" that overcame me as the morning wore on. Yes, I was absolutely terrified as one horrible thing after another happened to me, not knowing if I'd be alive to see the end of that day. However, what overtook that fear was this "calmness" I began to feel. Just as Jesus describes to Mack in your book (The Shack), it DID take the Trinity to get me calm and assure me that everything was going to be OK somehow. How would you know about such peace? Only people who have "been there" in those kinds of circumstances know what it's like to have the peace of Jesus in you when hell is happening to you. Even while I was being shot, God still reached down and had His hand over my soul, telling it to stay in my body and reassuring my soul that He had placed it in a body that would be able to withstand what was happening to it.*

Maggie survived and went on to compete in high school and collegiate athletics, in spite of three bullets permanently lodged in her body.

Suffering! Is love without suffering even possible?

At first glance the answer would seem to be no, because who among us has not experienced the entwining of love and suffering? It seems that every risk of love involves the looming potential—if not inevitability—of loss, with all its attendant suffering. We are surrounded and engulfed in it—with our parents and children, in our friendships and acquaintances. And blaring from the news headlines and subtexts, we witness racial and gender inequity and the plight of the poor. And these themes are central to the stories we see in theaters and our many screen devices. Suffering! It is everywhere . . . and so is love. In a world that is divided ideologically, religiously, politically, ethnically, socially, financially, etc., we as human beings share at least these two things in common: love and loss. And so love and suffering seem inextricably woven together. So back to our question: *Can love exist without suffering?*

Another dear friend called me yesterday, and we talked about the seeming inundation of trials and difficulties that surround us in our families and friendships. Cancer, mental illness, death, financial upheaval, relational disintegration—the litany seemed endless. She and I have a common religious history in which spirituality was often couched in militaristic terms. We were told that we were caught in an unseen spiritual war in which we are mostly on the defensive, looking for the right magic words and formulas to make it stop, let alone win. I am not saying that spiritual battles do not exist— they do—but often it is easier to blame dark forces than own the darkness that we as human beings have brought to the table. My friend asked, "Is this a specific attack? Is it because we are a praying people that all hell is breaking loose?"

"No," I said. "These losses are everywhere. We are surrounded by distress that is common to broken humanity. They usually have no specific focus on us. We are not suffering because we are better or worse than others; we experience pain and loss because we live in a broken world made up of human beings who are just like us. Besides," I continued, "we are getting older, and our relational frame of reference has expanded and deepened, as has our presence in the midst of loss. I think such suffering is incarnational. Because Jesus dwells within us as we are present to the hurts and losses of our broken world, we are participating with and in God" (John 14:20).

So . . . can love exist without suffering?

Yes! Prior to Creation, love without suffering was always present in the relationship of the Father, Son, and Holy Spirit. Suffering is not intrinsic to love. Submission is intrinsic to love, but not suffering. Loss and suffering were introduced into the cosmos by us human beings, and because we are created in Christ, suffering was utterly embraced by God.

In the shadow of Adam's independent turning from Life, he introduced death into the cosmos. As we each in our choices and actions continue to turn from Life, we reaffirm the profound hold that death has on us. Death is always accompanied by suffering. But God refuses to be absent from the Creation and infuses our suffering with Presence and Love.

In general terms, the global community of followers of Jesus makes up about a third of humanity. When we enter into Resurrection Weekend (Easter), you can almost hear the collective breath being held.

On Good Friday, death takes humanity by the throat. But Life reaches out and pulls death into a relentless embrace, drawing it down into Life, where it is extinguished by Love. Saturday, in the valley of the shadow of death, Jesus plunders the place of the dead, and Resurrection morning raises all of humanity in His Life.

As God encounters our humanity, God also enters our suffering, and as we experience suffering, we encounter the humanity of others. The miracle is that life springs out of death, the flower breaks through concrete, and beauty arises out of ashes.

God refuses to be absent from the Creation and infuses our suffering with Presence and Love.

In my life there has been suffering I neither wanted nor had control over. Things, such as my childhood innocence, were stolen from me. I also experienced suffering that I brought on myself and dumped on the people around me. Being broken myself, I, too, began to break things. Suffering is an invitation to be real and also to identify with humanity, and it is a fire that will burn away the false so that the true might emerge.

In *The Shack,* Mackenzie spends a weekend having his world unraveled, and from the depths of his suffering comes transformation, not only for himself but also extending to everyone in his world. That weekend represents eleven years of my life. Who would have thought that the work of dismantling the brokenness of my own personal shack would result in an unexpected book that has touched the lives of so many around this planet? Would I ever want to go through that process again? Absolutely not! But I am grateful every day for how suffering changes me, allowing me to more fully participate inside the losses of others and become more free to love, to become more alive and human.

In our temporal experience, Love cannot exist without suffering until the last vestiges and hints of death are fully eradicated. May we who are growing in our relationship with Jesus choose to be present in the midst of the sufferings of others as well as in our own, and thereby participate in the abiding and active Love of God.

23

"You will never find God in a box."

I have a religious heritage. Some of it was profoundly helpful, truly. Parts of it were devastating and had to be unwound and unlearned. There were also some elements of being raised inside this box that seemed unfortunate at the time but later turned out to be part of an emerging good. Let me give an example.

I paid my own way through college, with the help of scholarships, grants, the kindness of a few, and good old-fashioned work. My family was not financially able to help. They prayed. In retrospect, it was more than enough.

My first three undergraduate years were spent at an accredited Bible college in Saskatchewan, western-central

Canada, where I was working toward a degree in theology. Although it may sound completely counterintuitive, I found employment at CKCK Radio in Regina as a six-to-midnight rock-and-roll disc jockey to help pay tuition and expenses. The school looked the other way, in part because I was a high achiever and in part because I was a Third-Culture Kid, a Missionary Kid from their denomination.

But I never graduated from that school. At the end of my third year, even though I was president of the junior class and involved in athletics and community, when the list of scholarships and grants were posted, my name was conspicuously absent. There were three basic qualifications for the money: scholastic achievement (check), financial need (check), and spiritual maturity (uh . . . check?). Some of my friends went to the school administration to ask if this was an oversight. The administration's response was "We have determined that Paul is not a good investment for the denomination."

They were right. I wasn't a good investment. So I didn't graduate from that institution. Instead, I went up into the wilds of northern Alberta and the Syncrude

"You will never find God in a box."

oil mining project, a six-thousand-man camp where I earned enough to pay all debts and build some reserves. From there, on my way to Los Angeles to continue my education, I reached a crossroads in Oregon, met a woman, and have lived here ever since. Part of the backhanded grace of that school's decision was that I am married to Kim, something for which I will be forever grateful. But it was years before I again set foot inside a doorway of my own denomination.

I grew up in a world of boxes: *us and them, in and out, worthy and unworthy, believer and unbeliever, saved and unsaved,* and on and on. Boxes. Cages. Those Pentecostals. Those Baptists. Those Muslims. Those New Agers. Those Taoists. We create myriad of ways to categorize and keep each other at a distance or to discount or marginalize or use or manipulate. And with those boxes, we create identities for ourselves based on generalizations and innuendo.

But religion doesn't have a corner on the market when it comes to building boxes. Social culture, politics, science, economic systems—they all do this. At times boxes are helpful and necessary. They are helpful when it comes to clarifying that an illness is flu and not a brain tumor. At other times, boxes and categories lead to the horrific—diabolical genocide and abuse, for instance. Sadly, some of these catastrophic things are done in the name of God or humanism or plain old greed. We forget that the human being is always more important than the category.

When readers tell me that my writing has helped them take God out of the box, I understand what they are saying. I am thrilled that what I have offered has shaped the holy ground of their story and has challenged potentially false imaginations about God and creation, including our humanity.

But we have to be careful when we leave boxes behind. When we leave one box, we are frequently tempted to construct and climb into a new one. It is easy to become smug and self-righteous all over again and to refer to the precious people who are still inside the boxes we recently left as "those" people. We unwittingly continue to participate in dividing human beings into classifications for management and judgment. Worse, we might assume that God abandoned that box when we did and that "those" people exist in a space where God is no longer active.

Our arrogance is that we could craft something, a box, that can keep God out. God has never been a respecter of the boxes we build. It almost seems that God treats our precious boxes as though they weren't real. Imagine that! Worse, when we want God to put the heavenly housekeeping seal of approval on our box, God has the audacity to go and hang out with the people in that "other" box. The nerve! The truth is, whatever aspects of true freedom that have become a part of my life are always attended by a greater capacity to love, to accept, to enfold, to respect.

I have learned many things in life and some of them are profound, at least to me. Here is one of them, a simple statement that time and again reminds me of a

"The only time we will find God in a box is because God wants to be where we are."

bigger picture: "The only time we will find God in a box is because God wants to be where we are." And that is all the time.

201

By the way, that school I told you about, the one that I didn't graduate from? Well, a couple of decades after I left, it closed its doors and reopened as a brand-new modern campus in Alberta. I was their first speaker.

God is the source of all humor, don't you agree? After I spoke and told this same story, a young man walked up to me grinning, tatted, and pierced. "Well," he laughs, "things have changed a lot around here."

"Yeah," I responded, and gave him a hug. "Haven't we all."

24

"Not everyone is a child of God."

Here is the basic question: Is every human being a child of God or only certain ones?

Through my friend Jim Henderson, I met Matt Casper at a writers' conference in San Diego. Matt is a declared atheist. One of the first things he told me was "Paul, you know I am an unbeliever, right?"

"No, you're not," I replied.

"Yes, I am," he insisted, almost as if I had offended him.

"Look," I offered. "Belief is an activity, not a category. Anyway, I come from the people who made up that category, and, frankly, most of us struggle with belief and trust. We haven't been able to find the believe-o-meter, the gadget you attach to your head or heart that tells you how much you are believing and whether it is enough to be 'in.'"

For a second, he looked at me blankly but then laughed. "What are you talking about?"

I laughed, too. "It doesn't really matter. So, tell me, Matt, what do you believe in?"

"You want to know what I believe in? Most people want to talk to me about what I don't believe in. Let me think." He paused before answering. "I believe in the way I love my children. Paul, I didn't know I had the capacity to love like this until I had my own children. Without question I would step in front of a bullet for them, or take their hurts to myself if I could."

"So, Matt, you obviously aren't talking about romantic love. Would it be accurate to describe this love you believe in as other-centered, self-giving?"

"That is exactly what it is."

We talked for the better part of an hour. Turns out Matt not only believes in Love, but in Life and in Truth. Not bad for an unbeliever.

"Not everyone is a child of God."

But does that make him a child of God?

No, it doesn't. He already was a child of God.

I can hear someone at the back of the room say, "Well, everyone is a child of God in the sense that everyone is created by God, but . . ."

. . . and now comes the rationalization and justification for creating another box, another way to divide people into categories of value.

In our family, our children assume, and rightly so, that they are . . . our children. They belong *with* us because they are expressions *of* us. Their very existence is the only requirement for being our child. They don't have to do anything to become more our child, and nothing they can do will disqualify them from being fully our child. And furthermore, they don't have to believe they are our children in order to make it true. Even if one of our children decided to never speak to us again, that choice would not have the power to change their fundamental identity as son or daughter. Would it impact our relationship? Yes. Would it change their identity? No. They can deny that they are our son or daughter; they could even go to court and have their name changed.

Sorry, but they are not powerful enough to change the truth of who they are, even though their choices will affect their experience of that relationship.

In the New Testament, Acts 17:28–29, Paul the Apostle writes that "in God we live and move and exist, as even some of your own poets have said, 'For we also are God's children.' Being then the children of God . . ." And in Ephesians 4:5–6, "One Lord, one faith, one baptism; *one God and Father of all,* who is over all and through all and *in all*" (emphasis added).

> *Every human being you meet, interact with, react and respond to, treat rudely or with kindness and mercy: every one is a child of God.*

Every human being you meet, interact with, react and respond to, treat rudely or with kindness and mercy: every one is a child of God. If we considered that we are all together members of one family, might we care for one another with more consideration and kind intention? Every human being is my brother, my sister, my mother, my father . . . a child of God.

A couple of years ago, I got a call from Matt. He

wanted to know if I would write the foreword for a book that he and Jim were writing together called *Saving Casper*.

"You need to know that I am still an atheist," he said.

"That's okay," I responded. "I am still a Canadian."

The foreword I submitted to the publisher was re-written and sent back. It made me chuckle. I emailed Jim and Matt letting them know that. "Perhaps I am not the right person for this project," I said, and I offered to bow out.

Sweet Matt thought I had been hurt by the response of the publisher and called me, both to encourage me and to look for a way to bridge the differences. In that conversation he said something with the purest of heart and intention that made me laugh but also shake my head: "Paul, Jim and I both love your original fore-word; and while we don't agree with the publisher, we think there is a way to find middle ground. You have to remember—we are dealing with Christians. It's baby steps."

Indeed!

Do you see what has happened in the course of this

little chapter? Do you feel it? Matt Casper, an atheist, has become human to you. He is a good man, who loves his children, who believes in Love and Life and Truth, who is witty and kind and generously compassionate.

Jim has a saying: "Relationship breaks the rules." He is right. When someone becomes a human being rather than a category or box, everything changes. What if we not only see one another as human but also regard the other as a loved child of God?

25

"God is disappointed in me."

Most of us know what it's like to feel the devouring abyss of disappointment, especially in the face and voice of others. Every child yearns to hear "I am proud of you," not for performance but simply for *being*. The following statements resonate powerfully and have tremendous impact:

> *You belong to me and I belong to you.*
> *The universe is better because you are in it.*
> *I love you.*
> *I am especially fond of you.*

My father was disappointed in me—all the time. At least that is what I felt as a child and therefore what I believed. Whether or not he was, I don't really know. We have not had that conversation yet.

There are many ways to shame a child, and sadly, many of us know this from experience. Cruel words and harsh declarations of judgment unhinge little souls from their moorings:

You are disgusting.
You're just a slut.
You will never amount to anything.
You're an idiot.
After all we have done for you . . .
I was happy until you came along.
I wanted a boy.
I wish you had never been born.

Then there is the utter dismantling that happens through sexual abuse, where the fabric of the soul is shredded by boundary-smashing, wrongful distortions of intimacy. The cognitive dissonance, where a child has to hold completely conflicting values and beliefs, can be so profound that the mind creates alternative and disassociated personas to house the overwhelming clashes and secrets raging within the self, made even more confusing by abusers who ought to be trusted.

Children who are exposed to these sorts of lies either will find a way to survive—through violence toward others, self-punishment, or addiction's enticing momentary escapes—or will curl up somewhere and die. Everything wrong in the world, they believe, is their fault. Abused children cannot process that their parents may be flawed or are in the midst of loss themselves or might not even possess the capacity to love without damaging. Often an abused child believes that the rage poured out is deserved and that the heart-shredding words are true.

But there is another devastating way to shame a child, and that is through *silence*. The turned-away face and the little shake of the head before the door closes leave a child absolutely and utterly alone—crushed under the voiceless glance of disappointment.

I must have been about six years old when my mother coerced my father into taking me on one of his mission treks into the jungle. It was my first and, even though I could sense his anger, perhaps I hoped I could win him over. As soon as we were out of sight of the compound, he took off without a word, leaving me trying to run fast enough to catch up, crying and crying and crying. I remember that day as if it were yesterday—the white dot of his shirt disappearing and reappearing and getting smaller each time. I have no memory of ever finding him. The devastation of being unacceptable felt final.

I didn't know that my mother suffered from depression. All I knew was that her door would close, and we would hear her cry. Sometimes she would disappear for a few months at a time. I was the eldest, and I felt keenly that her sadness was my fault. I knew I was a disappointment.

For many, life itself is a series of disappointments. Things don't turn out the way we had wished. Circumstances seem to work against us or something comes out of nowhere and knocks down what we had worked hard to build. The unexpected washes it away as quickly as a hurricane, a flood, or a political, business, or moral decision.

As we mature, we begin to discern the difference between *disappointment* and *grief*. *Grief* is a healthy response to loss. In addition to grieving the loss of someone we love, we may also experience grief when a desire or hope or prayer is not fulfilled in the way we had imagined, or seemingly not at all. And sometimes our grief is expressed as regret, by which we own and understand our participation in the losses of our lives, especially the losses we inflicted on others. Grief is embedded in real life, real loss.

Disappointment largely revolves around expectations and imagination. I expect you to act a certain way, or I expect a specific outcome, or I expected to have achieved (fill in the blank) by now, or I expected that my life would be different or that I would be working in a field that I actually like. Fueled by media images, expectations are mostly disappointments waiting to happen and almost entirely built on imagination or illusion. Now, I understand the positive power of visualization and the neurological benefits of meditation, but that is not what I am talking about. I'm talking about imagining outcomes that can't or don't materialize.

This is precisely why God is never disappointed in you. God has no such imaginations or illusions. God knows you, completely, fully, and with unrelenting affection. You don't surprise God. God delights in you, as you delight in your own children; God also grieves for and with you when you act inside your lies and darkness—*but not because God expected more of you*. God is a fully engaged participant, present in the deepest and most profound

> *God is never disillusioned by you; God never had any illusions about you in the first place.*

activities happening inside the highest of all creation— you. God knows you for who you truly are and grieves for the distance between that truth and what you believe about yourself. It is from that gap of darkness and lies that we project God's disappointment and abandonment.

God is never disillusioned by you; God never had any illusions about you in the first place.

God is never disappointed in you; God has no expectations.

"God is disappointed in me."

Do you remember the verses halfway through Psalm 22? That's the psalm that begins with "My God, my God, why have you forsaken me." This was the cry of Jesus when He experientially entered all of humanity's lies and darkness, when He plunged into the shadow depths in which we projected a turned-away face of God. We believe that we are abandoned and unworthy to be face-to-face with God, and it is in that delusion that Jesus finds us. Halfway through this psalm, which Jesus knew by heart, are these words:

> *You do not despise the afflictions of the afflicted one,*
> *Nor will you turn your face from him,*
> *And when he cries, you will hear.*

This God does not do abandonment. We will never be powerful enough to make God's face turn from us. Because God knows us utterly and is with us always—*you* are never a disappointment.

26

"God loves me for my potential."

I love music. Music has always had the power to reach places in me that other things could not find. How many times throughout my life did she gently slip by my mental guards and dissociative survival skills and catch me by surprise, tapping into emotions that normally are safely secure behind the steely doors of my heart? The 1970s opened up a whole new world for me: Carole King's *Tapestry*, Jackson Browne's *Saturate Before Using*, Bruce Cockburn's *Sunwheel Dance* (with songs like "Fall," "He Came from the Mountain," and "Dialogue with the Devil"), Larry Norman's *So Long Ago the Garden*, Dylan, the Moody Blues, the Beatles, Leonard Cohen, and so many others.

The presence of these poets and musicians also helped ease a great loss: my love for the piano. When I was barely a teenager, I was already playing tenth-grade-level classical music (a standard set by the Royal Conservatory of Music, in Toronto), which at that time would have qualified me to teach. But I couldn't sight-read; it was almost as if I had a mental block. I could memorize a fifteen-page Tchaikovsky piece without any trouble but couldn't play a hymn from sheet music.

Over the span of two years, my teacher entered me in two large music festivals, the highest prizes being full scholarships to places like Juilliard. Both years I came in second. Both years to Beethoven's *Moonlight Sonata*. For a week after each failure, I threw up constantly. My teacher had great plans for me, saw immense "potential" in me, and pushed me toward the perfection necessary to reach the top.

In order to survive, I quit. Stone-cold quit. Walked away and have rarely touched a piano in the forty-six years since. The pressure of others' expectations regarding my potential was too much to bear—especially in the face of repetitive failure. The embarrassment of quitting was not as high a price as the inevitable disaster that I felt loomed on the horizon. For those of us who live with shame, every compliment is a new expectation, an inevitable disappointment waiting to happen, a new way to fail. My teacher disappeared along with my potential.

Over the years, I have coached each of our six children in some form of athletics and am now the assistant coach serving one of our sons, who is head coach for our six-year-old grandson's basketball team. It is akin to herding cats with their tails on fire, and utterly delightful . . . most of the time. Sadly, it is common to witness parents projecting huge expectations on their kids—wanting them to fulfill their "potential" and be the very best.

Interestingly, sports offer an outlet for greater authenticity than many religious services. At a sporting event people get real crazy. They are emotional, expressive; they sing, dance, feel like they belong; they violate all manners of social customs and norms and participate in ways that you rarely see in a religious environment.

There is an honesty in sports that emerges in few other scenarios. The thrill of competition and the joy of participation and community create almost magical moments, and the intricacy and quality of the game itself brings out a rare abandon. But in sports we also see the darker side of humanity clawing its way to the surface. The competition of life outside the arena expresses itself inside. The fear of failure, low self-esteem hiding barely beneath the surface of civility, the need to win: all are soon evident in the emotional displays that so easily explode after a bad call or an unfair decision.

Our grandson is six in a league of six-to-eight-year-olds. This is his first experience with basketball, and he is having the time of his life. He was born prematurely, all of four pounds and half an ounce, and is easily the smallest player on our team. We have one semicoordinated player who can dribble the ball the length of the court, which helps. But our goal for the season is that the boys have such a great time that they want to play again next year.

Even with players so young, some of the parents—especially the fathers—already have too much at stake. We don't officially keep score in our league. We made one basket our first game and two, I think, in our second game, but we had great fun! Even so, I can see the desperation in the faces of some of the dads, imagining their son as the next Michael Jordan. They try to encourage, but end up yelling, shaming, and communicating to their sons that their acceptability is linked to their performance, which is dependent on them fulfilling their potential. Sadly, there are often two things at risk: the father's sense of worth and the son's sense of knowing he is loved regardless.

"Fulfilling your potential"—now, there is a moving target. No one knows what that means for you or me, so it can't actually be defined by anyone. It's an easy "fail." Potential always seems to be determined by someone else, even though it is part of the mystery that is stored in the person who is "you."

Does God love me because of my potential? No! Do I love my children because of their potential? No! If I am not yet "enough," when will I be? How are we to enjoy our children in the present if the focus is on some future potential that qualifies the value of each moment? How will our children play?

Some people, including me, used to read Proverbs 22:6 as a principle of discipline. "Train up a child in the way that they should go and when they are old they will not depart from it." We were wrong. The Hebrew is actually an encouragement to parents and caregivers. "Train up a child in *their* way [that is, in that child's unique way] . . ." Each child has "their" way, because each child is an incredible one-of-a-kind tapestry of being.

> *How are we to enjoy our children in the present if the focus is on some future potential that qualifies the value of each moment?*

Do I want my child to be "everything he or she can be"? Of course, but I have no idea whatsoever what that will look like or how it will be expressed.

There is no end goal for us, no finally "arriving," no reaching the place of potential success. We are all eternal beings who are completely loved at every point along the way, and regardless of what our journey looks like, we are relentlessly loved inside every part of the process of this life.

Yes, I will put my strength and energy into that

"God loves me for my potential."

which is front of me, but not because it will help me reach my potential. There is no "potential" competition when it comes to being loved. However, there is a celebration, a joyful participation that allows me to hear and express the constant presence of the music that used to only occasionally find her way into my heart and soul.

27

"Sin separates us from God."

I often talk to people whose hearts have been broken open by *The Shack*. Sometimes they are ready to believe again but think they can't be in relationship with God because of some behavior or shame in their past. They feel hopeless and separated. The irony is that the healing for their sadness is always within their reach, because their actions never had the power to separate them from God in the first place.

If no one else tells us that we are failing to live up to God's behavioral expectations, we often preach the message to ourselves.

Let's start with something simple. Mistakes are an essential part of being human.

Eight-year-old grandson G was having a conversation with his father, our son.

G: Dad, do you think Jesus ever made a mistake?
Dad: Well, G, very smart people have had different thoughts about that question. What do you think?
G (*after reflecting*): I think he did, because how could he have ever learned anything if he didn't?

G is learning that making mistakes is not only *okay* for human beings but is also indeed essential. Expecting perfection is a denial of our humanity, as if making mistakes or not knowing something or forgetting the right answer is the same as sinning. Do we really think that Jesus never made a mistake on His homework, or never forgot someone's name, or as a carpenter always made accurate measurements? Jesus didn't have a reputation for being the "best carpenter" in Nazareth, making perfect doors and always-level tables.

Jesus is fully human. What do you think Scripture means when it says, "Jesus grew in wisdom and stature before God and Man"? Jesus wasn't always completely wise—He *grew* in wisdom. Errors made in any learning process are then incorporated into the maturing of a person.

Now stay with me here. In Jesus's humanity, there were certain things He didn't know. He didn't know about *Star Wars* or Schrödinger's cat or Heisenberg's uncertainty principle. When he cried as a baby or stubbed his toe or misspelled a word, He did so because He is human. He asked for help because he needed it (like when He asked His disciples to get a boat ready for Him). He made the constant choice to trust God because He knew He was a human being in relationship with God; He knew the truth of His being.

Pride is a sin because it is a denial of being human. Humility is always a celebration of being human. *Please forgive me. I made a mistake. I was wrong. I didn't listen. May I ask a question? I didn't know. I realize now that I hurt you. I am learning myself. I am open to being wrong.*

What about active rebellion, betrayal, and hurting others or ourselves? Is that not sin? What if sin isn't fundamentally about behavior, but something deeper?

LIES WE BELIEVE ABOUT GOD

What if it is so deep that all the behavior modification and moralistic performance won't even begin to address it? What if our focus on behavior is an attempt to treat the symptoms and distracts us from attending to the actual disease?

The Greek word often translated into the English as "sin" is *hamartia*. A moralist will tell you that the word means "missing the mark" and then go on to explain that the mark is "moral perfection" or "right behavior," and once again we are back on the performance hamster wheel. But if the essence of God's nature is relationship, then sin must be defined and understood as missing a relational reality, a distortion of the image of God in us.

> *If the essence of God's nature is relationship, then sin must be defined and understood as missing a relational reality, a distortion of the image of God in us.*

Hamartia is made up of two parts: *ha-* (an aspirated alpha), which is a negation (like *un-* or *dis-*), and *-martia*, from the Greek root *meros*, which means "form, origin, or being." The fundamental meaning is "negation of origin or being" or "formlessness."

Yes, it is about "missing the mark," but the mark is not perfect moral behavior. The "mark" is the Truth of your being.

There is a truth about who you are: God's proclamation about a "very good creation" is the truest about *you*. That very good creation is the form or origin of you, the truth of who you are in your being. Sin, then, is anything that negates or diminishes or misrepresents the truth of who you are, no matter how pretty or ugly that is. Behavior becomes either an authentic way of expressing the truth of your good creation or an effort to cover up (performance behavior) the shame of what you think of yourself (worthless).

And what does the truth of your being look like? God. You are made in the image of God, and the truth of your being looks like God.

You are patient.
You are kind.
You are good.
You are humble.
You are forgiving.
You are a truth teller.

You are trustworthy.

You have integrity.

You are long-suffering.

You are loving.

You don't keep a record of wrongs.

You desire the best.

You treat others the way in which you would want to be treated.

You are furious at everything that is wrong.

You are pure of heart . . .

And so on.

These are all expressions of the truth of our being.

Difficult to believe, right?

I think that is the point.

And this brings us to separation. Does sin separate us from God?

Separation is the fundamental building block of religion. Once you assume separation, you are at the mercy of any and every good-intentioned or evilly intentioned person who has found the "secret" formula to getting across the chasm to God. Once division and separation are established as real, entire religious systems, institutions, and hierarchies can be built as the path to salvation or enlightenment, and people will pay blood, sweat, tears, and money to get from the damned side to the saved.

We Christians have long espoused a theology of separation. A lot of "my people" will believe that the following statement is in the Bible, but it isn't: *"You have sinned, and you are separated from God."*

We think it is obviously true because we have believed it our entire lives. Once you believe this lie, the implications are devastating and the questions unanswerable. How does one get unseparated? If I do the right things, say the right words, have enough faith, pray the right prayers, will I be transported across the great divide and made part of the "special" people?

And it gets ever more confusing and complicated. How do you really know you are "in" or "across"? Is it temporary? What about those I love? What if people don't know how to get unseparated? It is easy, then, to posit that Jesus came to get us unseparated, but even then we can't agree on what that means and how He did it or for whom.

If separation is a lie, does it mean that no one has ever been separated from God? That is exactly what it means. Nothing can separate us from the love of God (Romans 8:38–39).

Jesus did not come to build a bridge back to God or to offer the possibility of getting unseparated. One of the multifaceted purposes of the incarnation of Jesus is that we who are lost in the delusion of separation can witness a human life who knows He is not.

There is "nothing" outside God. There is only God, and Creation is created "in" God; and according to John 1, Creation is specifically created "inside" Jesus, the Word who is God (see verses 3–4).

If Jesus is actually and historically God fully joining us in our humanity—permanently and intentionally— then Jesus is God comfortable in His own skin. He is God in the midst of our blood, sweat, tears, brokenness, and blindness.

Do we really think that we are powerful enough, even in our most horrific actions and denial of our own humanity, to push God away? Do we think we can be so wretched and sinful that we become abhorrent to

"Sin separates us from God."

God? Some of us do. Some of us can't even look in a mirror because we are so ashamed of ourselves. Some of us cut ourselves and do self-harm because we believe we deserve it or because in our bleeding we might feel something real.

Meanwhile, God is watching . . . from a distance?

No!

There is no separation.

28

"God is One alone."

I have written most of my life, even as a boy. I wrote to get my inside world out. I wrote in an effort to understand. I wrote to discern the thoughts of others who impacted my life. Over the years, words were the gifts I gave family and friends—poems, short stories, and songs—through which I said, "I love you!" and "You matter to me."

As I've mentioned before, I wrote *The Shack* at the request of my wife, Kim. She asked me to put what I thought in one place—as a gift to our children.

I did not feel whole enough to attempt what she'd asked until the year I turned fifty. When we gain some distance and are able to look back at our lives, we see sig-nificant milestones that we often blundered through with little thought or awareness. When I wrote the book, I had finally reached a place of contentment in my life. I had no secrets. I had no image to maintain, largely because I had no secrets. I had no addictions, and I was comfortable inside my own skin for the first time in my life. I wasn't writing to impress or succeed or become all that I was intended to be. I didn't create with an agenda or with any intent that what I wrote would be "used" by God. I wrote as a gift to our six children. I wanted to say to them, "Let me tell you about the God who actually showed up and healed my broken heart, not the god I grew up with in my modern evangelical Christian fundamentalism."

I penned much of the story on the commuter train, forty minutes each way to one of my three jobs. Long-hand, on yellow legal pads. Beginning with questions and responses, I wrote conversations between me and God about any topic in which I thought my kids might be interested. It wasn't long before I had stacks of notes. I remember thinking, *I could call this "Conversations with God,"* and just as the thought went through my mind, I looked out the train window to see a marquee for a movie opening called *Conversations with God*. Oh well.

But I did start thinking about story. Who doesn't like a good story? And what better way to wrap what I was hoping to communicate? Every human being is a story, so we all have a natural affinity for story. But who would be asking these questions, and why? That was when Mackenzie Allen Phillips was born—a man who could house my doubts, my fears, my wonder, and my own journey toward wholeness.

When I am asked how I could write something for my children that involved the loss of a character like Missy, Mack's five-year-old daughter, who is abducted, I reply that such a tragedy asks the best questions. I would rather that we didn't live in a world where such horrific losses could be perpetrated, but we do. Our own niece had been killed the day after her fifth birthday. What if something like this, or similar, happened to a grandchild? What if I weren't there? What would I want to say to my own children in the face of such heartbreak? And thus *The Shack* came to be.

So how does one face this worst of tragedies: the loss between a parent and a child? Frankly, I can't comprehend how families who have no sense of faith and hope even begin to walk their way through such darkness. While the activity of evil raises a million questions, the God I grew up with was of little comfort. In fact, that God was considered the originator of evil, a distant deity who had a plan that included the torture of a child. One can't run to God if God is the perpetrator.

If you have read the novel, you know that Mackenzie believes in the god who is one alone. God the Father was a distant deity, hidden and holy, a darkness somewhere behind Jesus, and different in character than Jesus. That God was usually disappointed, if not angry, was unknowable, unreachable, and was watching from the infinite distance of a disapproving heart. That God was the one whom Mack went to meet in the shack, but when that one was a no-show, Mack lost it, destroying the place with the fury of a father bereft and a lover betrayed.

The reason that this one-alone God did not show up is that this one-alone God does not exist, except in our minds darkened by religious indoctrination and our own pain. That God has no answer for us. In some perverted scenarios, Jesus comes to protect us from that God's vengeance or just retribution. That God needs to be appeased, and failure is met by wrath and judgment.

If God has ever been alone, there would be neither a basis in the universe for love nor a framework for relationship. Love is other-centered and self-giving, but if there was no "other" in the beginning and God was alone, then God cannot be Love. Merciful, perhaps, but not Love.

This is why the triune God matters to me. Yes, I believe in *One* God, but this One God is the relationship of Three Persons, who have been forever in the great dance of face-to-face-to-face. This divine dance is full of life and light and music and laughter and joy and wonder and submission and goodness. Theirs is the mutual interpenetration of One with the Other without any diminishment or absorption of Person. This is the grand celebration of relationship in which all creation is created. This is a God who *is* Love—a God who cannot be anything that is not Love.

And frankly, I don't need a God who knows how to be alone. When I am in the middle of devastation and loss, I need a God who knows how to be *with*.

> *I don't need a god who knows how to be alone. When I am in the middle of devastation and loss, I need a God who knows how to be* with.

So when God the Father comes bursting out from inside Mackenzie's shack, God the Father is not Gandalf with a bad attitude, not a distant white grandfather God, but Papa, an all-consuming fire of relentless affection wrapped in the person of a large black African woman. And She is not alone. With Her are Two, and the Three together are One.

"Then," Mack struggled to ask, "which one of you is God?"

"I am," said all three in unison.

A Catena

God's Drama of Redemption

A *catena*, in this case, is a chain of Scriptures (various translations based on the Greek New Testament) strung together as commentary on the theme of God's saving work for all—the grand arc of God's drama of redemption. When read aloud with a touch of gravitas, the momentum is powerful:

- And then *all* flesh shall see the salvation of God (Luke 3:6 NASB, emphasis mine).

- This man came for a witness, to bear witness of the Light, that through him *all* would believe (John 1:7 Aramaic Bible in Plain English/Greek NT, emphasis mine).

- Behold, the Lamb of God who takes away the sin of the *world* (John 1:29 NASB, emphasis mine).

- For God so loved the world that He gave His only begotten Son, that whoever believes in Him should not perish but have everlasting life. For God did not send His Son into the world to condemn the world, but to save the *world* through Him (John 3:16–17 KJV/NIV, emphasis mine).

- The Father loves the Son, and has given *all* things into His hand (John 3:35 AKJV, emphasis mine).

- We no longer believe because of what you said, for we have heard for ourselves and know that this really is the Savior of the *world* (John 4:42 Holman Christian Standard Bible, emphasis mine).

- For the bread of God is the bread that comes down from heaven and gives life to the *world* (John 6:33 NIV, emphasis mine).

- I am the light of the *world* (John 8:12 ESV, emphasis mine).

- And I, if I am lifted up from the earth, will draw [drag] *all* men to Myself (John 12:32 Berean Literal Bible/Greek NT, emphasis mine).

- Jesus knew that the Father had given *all* things into His hands (John 13:3 NIV/ESV, emphasis mine).

- *All* that the Father gives Me will come to Me, and the one who comes to Me I will by no means cast out . . . This is the will of the Father who sent Me, that of all He has given Me I should lose nothing, but should raise it up at the last day (John 6:37, 39 ESV, emphasis mine).

- For you granted him authority over *all* people that he might give eternal life to *all* those you have given him (John 17:2 NIV, emphasis mine).

- Heaven must receive him until the time comes for God to restore *all* things (Acts 3:21 NIV/Greek NT, emphasis mine).

- He made known to us the mystery of His will, according to His good pleasure which He purposed in

Himself, that in the dispensation of the fullness of the times He might gather together in one *all* things in Christ, both which are in heaven and which are on earth—in Him (Ephesians 1:9–10 AKJV, emphasis mine).

- And He put *all* things under His feet, and gave Him to be head over *all* things to the church, which is His body, the fullness of Him who fills *all* in *all*. (Ephesians 1:22–23 ESV, emphasis mine).

- For by grace we have been saved through faith, and this [faith] is not from yourselves, it is a gift of God, not of works, so that no one can boast (Ephesians 2:8–9 Aramaic Bible/Greek NT).

- He is the image of the invisible God, the firstborn over all creation. For *everything* was created by Him, in heaven and on earth, the visible and the invisible, whether thrones or dominions or rulers or authorities—*all* things have been created through Him and for Him. He is before *all* things, and by Him *all* things hold together . . . and through Him to reconcile *all* things to Himself by making peace through the blood of His cross—things on earth or things in heaven (Colossians 1:15–17, 20 Holman CSB/Greek NT, emphasis mine).

- As through one man's offense judgment came to *all* men, resulting in condemnation, even so through one Man's righteous act the free gift came to *all* men, resulting in justification of life (Romans 5:18 KJV/Greek NT, emphasis mine).

- For I am convinced that neither death, nor life, nor angels, nor principalities, nor things present, nor things to come, nor powers, nor height, nor depth, nor any other created thing, will be able to separate us from the love of God, which is in Christ Jesus our Lord (Romans 8:38–39 ESV).

- For from him and through him and to him are *all* things (Romans 11:36 NASV, emphasis mine).

- He has shut up *all* to unbelief so that he might have mercy on *all* (Romans 11:32 DBT/Greek NT, emphasis mine).

- For as in Adam *all* die, so also in Christ *all* will be made alive (1 Corinthians 15:22 NIV, emphasis mine).

- Then comes the end, when He hands over the kingdom to God the Father, when He abolishes all rule and all authority and power. For He must reign until He puts *all* His enemies under His feet. The last enemy to be abolished is death. For God has put everything under His feet. But when it says "everything" is put under Him, it is obvious that He who puts everything under Him is the exception. And when *everything* is subject to Christ, then the Son Himself will also be subject to the One who subjected everything to Him, so that God may be *all* in *all* (1 Corinthians 15:24–28 NASB/Holman CSB/Greek NT, emphasis mine).

- For God was in Christ reconciling the *cosmos* to Himself, not counting their sins against them (2 Corinthians 5:19 NIV/Greek NT, emphasis mine).

- At the name of Jesus *every* knee will bow—of those who are in heaven and on earth and under the earth—and *every* tongue should confess that Jesus Christ is Lord, to the glory of God the Father (Philippians 2:10–11 NASB, emphasis mine).

- He will transform the body of our humble condition into the likeness of His glorious body, by the power that enables Him to subject *all* things to Himself (Philippians 3:21 Holman CSB, emphasis mine).

- He desires *all* people to be saved and to come to the knowledge of the truth (1 Timothy 2:4 ESV, emphasis mine).

- We labor and strive for this, because we have put our hope in the living God, who is the Savior of *everyone*, especially of those who believe (1 Timothy 4:10 Holman CSB, emphasis mine).

- For the grace of God has appeared, bringing salvation to *all* people (Titus 2:11 ESV, emphasis mine).

- He appointed the Son heir of *all* things, and through whom also he made the universe. In these last days he has spoken to us by his Son, whom he appointed heir of *all* things (Hebrews 1:1–2 ESV/Greek NT, emphasis mine).

- He is not willing that *any* should perish but that *all* should come to repentance (2 Peter 3:9 KJV/Greek NT, emphasis mine).

- He Himself is the atoning sacrifice for our sins, and not only for ours, but also for those of the *whole* world (1 John 2:2 Berean Study Bible, emphasis mine).

- I heard *every* creature in heaven, on earth, under the earth, on the sea, and everything in them say: Blessing and honor and glory and dominion to the One seated on the throne and to the Lamb, forever and ever! (Revelation 5:13 Holman CSB, emphasis mine).

- Then He who sat on the throne said, "Behold, I make *all* things new" (Revelation 21:5 AKJV, emphasis mine).

A Final Word from Dietrich Bonhoeffer

"*In the body of Jesus Christ, God is united with humankind, all humanity is accepted by God, and the world is reconciled to God. In the body of Jesus Christ, God took on the sin of all the world and bore it. There is no part of the world, no matter how lost, no matter how godless, that has not been accepted by God in Jesus Christ and reconciled to God.*"

"*God loves human beings. God loves the world. Not an ideal human, but human beings AS THEY ARE; not an ideal world, but the REAL WORLD. What we find repulsive in their opposition to God, what we shrink back from with pain and hostility, namely, real human beings, the real world, this is for God the ground of unfathomable love. God establishes a most intimate unity with this. God becomes human, a real human being. While we exert ourselves to grow beyond our humanity, to leave the human behind us, GOD BECOMES HUMAN; and we must recognize that God wills that we be human, real human beings. While we distinguish between pious and godless, good and evil, noble and base, God loves REAL PEOPLE without distinction. God has no patience with our dividing the world and humanity according to our standards and imposing ourselves as judges over them. God leads us into absurdity by becoming a real human being and a companion of sinners, thereby forcing us to become the judges of God. God stands beside the real human being and the real world against ALL THEIR ACCUSERS. So God becomes accused along with human beings and the world, and thus the judges become the accused."*

Dietrich Bonhoeffer, *Ethics*
(New York: Touchstone, 1995), 66–68, 84–85

Acknowledgments

First, I want to express my gratitude for theologians throughout the centuries, especially the early church fathers and mothers. In reading their contributions, directly and indirectly, my view of Jesus has been enlarged and deepened. The book you hold in your hand is built on Christology, the question of who Jesus Christ is. Not a single chapter is unrelated to that theme. Most of the "lies" we believe about God arise out of inadequate and often pathetic apprehensions of the Person of Jesus. Because we often believe, sadly, in a very small Jesus, our view of humanity is even smaller.

ACKNOWLEDGMENTS

I am a blessed man, enfolded into layers of friendships and family that constantly enrich my life and remind me that we are each a significant expression of a wondrous and multifaceted humanity. I am surrounded by people who love me, but aren't impressed. Thank you!

Special thanks to Ami McConnell, Becky Nesbitt, and Philis Boultinghouse, who struggled with me through the editing process. Iron sharpens iron, if the angle is right. Also to Jonathan Merkh and the gang at Atria and Howard Books, thank you for your constant support and affection.

Thank you, Wes Yoder and Dan Polk, two friends who work side by side with me. Everything I create has your fingerprints on it somewhere.

To Jeni and Jay Weston, thank you, again, for giving me the space to work and write for days at a time. And thank you to my small group of readers—they know who they are—who see this material before you do, and because of their input it is better.

Finally, a very special thank-you to C. Baxter Kruger,

PhD, and John MacMurray, two friends whom I rely upon to help me think through the content of what I write. Your input has been repeatedly invaluable, made even more so by knowing that you love me as a brother.

Personal Notes

PERSONAL NOTES

PERSONAL NOTES

PERSONAL NOTES